Jim Munchbach, Agent, CPCU ChFC
1001 Pineloch, Suite 400
Houston, TX 77062
281 488 5075 Fax 281 280 9775
jim.munchbach.hlbi@statefarm.com

MAKE YOUR *Money* COUNT

CONNECTING YOUR RESOURCES TO WHAT MATTERS MOST

MAKE YOUR *Money* COUNT

CONNECTING YOUR RESOURCES TO WHAT MATTERS MOST

Jim Munchbach
With Patrick Springle
Foreword by Matt Chandler

WHAT LEADERS ARE SAYING ABOUT *MAKE YOUR MONEY COUNT*...

"As trusted advisors, we recognize that motivation is the key to change. In *Make Your Money Count,* Jim Munchbach provides powerful motivation to connect our finances with our purpose in life. This, I know, makes all the difference in the world. I enthusiastically recommend Jim's book."
—*Ron Blue, President, Kingdom Advisors*

"*Make Your Money Count* is a book for every person interested in a 'holistic' view of money, possessions and the abundant life. Jim Munchbach has effectively zeroed in on the critical elements of living our financial lives wisely. I fully expect this book will change the way you think about money, and I highly recommend it."
—*Dave Briggs, Director of the Stewardship Ministry at Willow Creek Community Church*

"Jim has a way of communicating simple, practical truths so they change our lives. His compelling writing style and stories breathe life and hope into our efforts to manage money. I recommend this book to people of all ages who want to be more intentional about their finances . . . and their lives."
—*Linda Miller, Global Liaison for Coaching, The Ken Blanchard Companies*

"More than any other book on the market, *Make Your Money Count* will help you align your money with your heart. With compelling stories and a practical 'blueprint,' Jim Munchbach will inspire and equip you to manage your finances with fresh vision and purpose."
— *Rick Baldwin, Senior Pastor, Friendswood Community Church, Friendswood, Texas, and author of* Fully Alive

"Jim should have titled the book *Make Your 'Life' Count* because he goes beyond showing you how to manage your finances. He opens our eyes to see what is really important in life—how money and investments can help us reach our life's goals."
—*Tom Wright, State Farm agent and author of* Stop Selling And Start Marketing

"This book shows you how to get complete control over your money and your life, develop a financial plan and achieve complete independence."
—*Brian Tracy, author of* The Way To Wealth

"Jim is a gifted communicator and has a heart for helping families in the area of financial management. His openness is a breath of fresh air in our industry. *Make Your Money Count* puts clear handles on the purpose and process of managing money, and I recommend it to all my clients."
—*Eric Brinley CFP®, Friendswood, Texas*

"The lure of money can be a cruel master. In his excellent book, Jim Munchbach helps us use our money to serve our highest purpose and achieve financial freedom."
—*Derric Johnson, Creative Consultant to Walt Disney World, author of nine books, musician, and pastor*

Copyright ©2007 by Jim Munchbach

All rights reserved. No part of this publication may be reproduced in any form, except for brief quotations in reviews, without the written permission of the publisher.

Formatting and cover design by Anne McLaughlin, Blue Lake Design, Dickinson, Texas.
Original artwork by Taylor Springle, Long Beach, California.
Proofed by Michelle Gooding, League City, Texas.
Published in the United States by Baxter Press, Friendswood, Texas.
Cover photos, © istockphoto.com
Image on page 99, © Dreamstime.com
Image on page 97, 103, 107, © istockphoto.com

ISBN: 1-888237-68-6
      978-1-888237-68-9

This book uses *The Message* by Eugene Peterson.
Scripture taken from *The Message*. Copyright © 1993, 1994, 1995, 1996, 2000, 2001, 2002. Used by permission of NavPress Publishing Group.

Certified Financial Planner Board of Standards Inc. owns the certification marks CFP®, CERTIFIED FINANCIAL PLANNER™ and federally registered CFP in the U.S., which it awards to individuals who successfully complete CFP Board's initial and ongoing certification requirements.

Printed in Canada

For Connie
(Proverbs 31:10-31)

We're ~~I'm~~ praying that God will use this book to make a difference in your life.

Jim & Connie

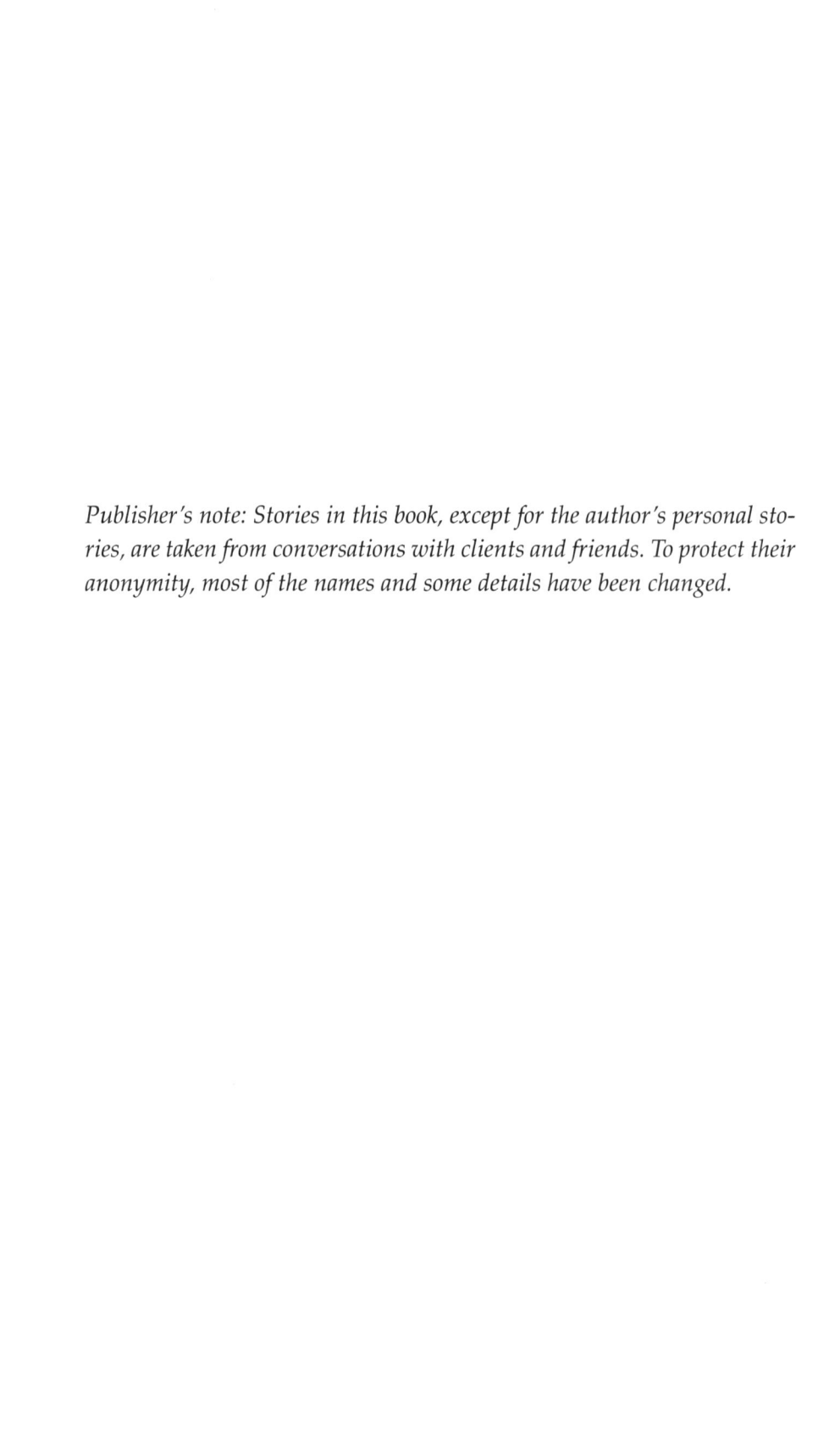

Publisher's note: Stories in this book, except for the author's personal stories, are taken from conversations with clients and friends. To protect their anonymity, most of the names and some details have been changed.

TABLE OF CONTENTS

Acknowledgements 13

Foreword 15

Introduction 17

Chapter 1   Your Heart's Desire 31

Chapter 2   First Memories about Money 49

Chapter 3   Powered by Purpose 69

Chapter 4   The Blueprint for Financial Success 91

Chapter 5   Putting It All Together 117

Chapter 6   Small Steps, Big Payoffs 145

Chapter 7   Tipping Points 157

Chapter 8   Pay It Forward 181

Appendices

    About the Author 207

    About Bridger Resources 209

    Resources 213

    Using *Make Your Money Count* in Groups and Classes 215

    To Order More Copies 219

ACKNOWLEDGEMENTS

A number of people have made significant contributions to this book, and I'm very grateful to each of them.

Bookstores are filled with titles that address money management, life planning, and fulfilling God's purpose for our lives, but very few combine all three into a single, powerful message. Several years ago, I talked to my friend Pat Springle about the possibility of producing a book like that. I wanted to write a book that helps people clarify their values, stimulates their passion to live for something bigger than themselves, and then connects their resources to those dreams. *Make Your Money Count* addresses far more than debt management. It helps every person take bold steps to use their money for things that really matter. In this book, Pat has helped me communicate ideas and principles in a fresh and powerful language designed to connect with all of us in a postmodern world.

For the past several years, I've been inspired by the teaching of Matt Chandler, pastor of The Village Church in Flower Mound, Texas. Matt communicates God's truth with passion and authenticity, and God uses his messages powerfully in my life. I'm honored that he wrote the foreword to my book.

In the same way, my pastor Rick Baldwin is a wonderful example of what this book is about. His heart for Christ, his powerful teaching, and his example are neon signs about the benefits of connecting our resources to what matters most.

I've known Taylor Springle for several years. He's a gifted young artist, and I'm happy to include some of his great illustrations in this book.

David Briggs is the Director of Willow Creek's Good Sense Stewardship Ministry which focuses on teaching, training and equipping people to live God-centered financial lives. David's insights and feedback during our final edits helped clarify the message of the book.

Finally, I want to thank all of the authors whose books have challenged my thinking and stimulated me to pursue God more passionately. I, and millions like me, will never be the same because these men and women communicate the life-changing message of what matters most—the love and grace of our Lord Jesus Christ.

Thank you, all.

FOREWORD

"All things are full of weariness; a man cannot utter it; the eye is not satisfied with seeing, nor the ear filled with hearing" (Ecclesiastes 1:8)

Could it be that you and I have been caught up in a bit of circular silliness? Let me explain what I mean. Tomorrow morning, the alarm will go off at 6:30, we will wake up, shower, get dressed, get in our car, stop at Starbucks to get our morning coffee, and then sit in traffic. We will eventually get to our office, our cubicle, even worse, our workstation (which just means we work in a closet). We will get there and work until lunch. At lunch, we will eat something, probably with some friends. Then after lunch, we will go back to our workstation, cubicle, office, shop, classroom, whatever, and we will work until 5:00 or 6:00. We will then leave work and maybe go to the gym but probably not. We will want to, we know we should, but instead, we'll go to dinner. We will eat dinner and go home to watch a little television and go to bed. Guess what the following day holds for us? Same thing. Same drink at Starbucks—nobody ever orders anything different. Maybe the same lunch. If it's different, it's one of three things you order from that restaurant. Back to the same office, same traffic, same television shows, same bed. Life is more like the film "Groundhog Day" than anyone wants to admit. This is what I mean by circular silliness—the predictable rut in which the majority of us feel captured.

So there are people, and maybe you're one of them, that pretend that their lives aren't in this predictable rut. Let me show you how they pretend. Ecclesiastes 1:9 says, "What has been is what will be, and what has been done is what will be done, and there is nothing new under the sun. Is there a thing of which it is said, 'See, this is new'? It has been already in the ages before us." Solomon, the writer of Ecclesiastes, is saying, "Listen, people like to pretend that their life isn't meaningless, that their life isn't stuck in a circular rut of boredom characterized by acquiring trinkets of all shapes and sizes and pretending that those trinkets are a new idea. In the end, they might have more color to them, but they're not new. There is nothing new."

Trinkets and new things are a deceptive part of the circular silliness that gets our minds away from the predictable, boring rut that defines our lives. Now if you're honest—and I'm not pretending that we are—you can see this play out in life over and over and over again. We obtain a gadget or a new bit of clothes or a new house or a new boat or a new car and immediately feel this indescribable relief and excitement to life. Have you ever thought about how strange that is? That it has this emotional effect on you? That a new cell phone—the cool one—actually makes you feel better? You get it and you just hold it. You admire it. When you're around people, you pull it out to check the time just so they can see. It is utterly amazing how an object can have such a profound effect on our worth. It's as if we're saying to ourselves, "This validates my existence."

Still, the Scriptures admonish us that trinkets are trinkets and nothing more. Nothing has changed. Okay, so your cell phone now has Windows on it instead of Palm, congratulations! You had a calendar six months ago. And guess what, thousands of years before that, Solomon had a calendar. There is nothing new under the sun and yet so many of us are going into debt and putting our money into places that have no real return on life, spirituality or advancing the eternal Kingdom that we find ourselves by the mercies of God belonging to.

My hope for you as you read Jim's book is that you would be saved from drowning in the ocean of shallow trivialities that has claimed the deep spiritual and emotional health of so many of us. In a chapter you read or a paragraph perused or maybe even a sentence written in the pages that follow, may Jesus save you from the lie that what you need for fulfillment and life is more of what you already possess. I pray that as this lie is exposed you might hear the Gospel call clearly over the crashing waves of perpetual consumption.

Matt Chandler
March, 2007

INTRODUCTION

"Ninety-eight percent of us will die at some point in our lives, so a little planning can go a long way." —*Ricky Bobby*, Talladega Nights

I could see it on their faces and hear it in their voices. The difference was startling. Two couples, both clients of mine, had daughters who were getting married, but that's where the similarities stopped. Chris and Robin wanted a nice wedding for their daughter Melissa, but Chris hadn't saved a dime since he started working after graduate school. He always figured "things would work out," and someone—his parents, his employer, or the lottery jackpot—would provide any money he and his family needed. But now, wedding plans were in full swing, and he had no money to pay for it. Money, or rather the lack of it, consumed him and his relationships with his wife and daughter. Over and over again, Robin and Melissa made plans, but when they presented them to Chris, he grimaced, shook his head, and then exploded, "You know we can't afford that! What are you thinking?"

Chris contacted me to ask for advice about managing his money, but in fact, he had no money to manage. The family had spent all they made every month since Chris and Robin got married, so there simply wasn't any money to pay for the wedding. As the reality of his past choices hit him in the face, Chris felt ashamed and humiliated because he wasn't able to provide for his dear daughter's needs. In a short time, his discouragement slipped into depression, and he felt completely hopeless, helpless, and worthless. Still, the wedding plans had to be made, and the stress between Chris and Robin robbed the family of the joy of Melissa's wedding. Eventually, Chris borrowed enough money to have a very modest ceremony, but the damage was done. Every moment and every decision was dominated by the painful lack of money, so relationships were strained. They endured, rather than celebrated, Melissa's wedding.

My other clients, Phil and Trish, had saved plenty of money for their daughter's wedding. No, they hadn't saved enough for swans, skywriters, and chateaubriand for 400, but they had enough for a beautiful wedding. Phil told me that a wonderful moment came early in the planning when his daughter Alicia asked, "Dad, what's our budget for the wedding?"

Phil answered with a question of his own, "How much were you thinking of?"

She gave him a number, and he replied, "You can add more to that. We have enough, and I want this to be a wonderful, beautiful day for you."

Imagine what that did for Alicia's sense of peace as she planned the wedding—and for her relationship with her dad!

I talked to Phil a number of times as the weeks wound down to the wedding, and each time, he told me some thing like, "Every day, I thank God that we have enough money to provide for Alicia's wedding. That takes such a load off. We're having a blast!"

Phil's family had some decisions to make, and of course, some of the choices were difficult ones. Should they allocate more money for a photographer and less for flowers, or the other way around? But the difficulty of those decisions pales in comparison to the shame, anger, and anxiety Chris, Robin, and Melissa experienced.

When Alicia's day arrived, it was a beautiful thing to see. Everybody was completely relaxed and focused on the joy of the moment, with no hint of anxiety about money. Phil told me, "Alicia's wedding was beautiful, fun, and meaningful. In fact, it was glorious!" Phil and Trish had been intentional about managing their money, and they experienced incredible benefits from their plan.

The Emotional Nature of Money

Money may seem inert, but it has the power to cripple or heal, to depress or inspire. Dr. Laurence Barton, the President and Chief Executive Officer of the American College, observed, "Money is tangible, but it is also emotional in nature. It is necessary for the exchange of goods and services, but is also what divides spouses and families and is often the source of permanent scars among loved ones. . . . Interestingly enough, many individuals spend more time analyzing the sports scores or their horoscope in the daily newspaper than they invest in monitoring their daily financial health."[1]

A recent study concluded that most decisions about money are emotional, not rational, decisions. We are inundated by countless messages that we simply have to have this product or that service to make us happy, successful, and accepted, but we don't hear many messages about the benefits of saving and investing. So we buy . . . hoping that this time our purchase will make us feel really good, but with a nagging sense of guilt and anxiety that we'll have to pay for it in another month. In a think tank sponsored by the National Endowment for Financial Education, a participant noted that most Americans now own things that only the wealthy would have enjoyed a few decades ago. But we're not paying for these things with cash—we're a credit society. He observed, "I think a lot of middle-income Americans are living their dreams. They're driving vehicles they can't afford and they're living in houses they can't afford. They have all the trappings. They're focused on what makes them happy today."[2]

> *A recent study concluded that most decisions about money are emotional, not rational, decisions.*

But other messages can touch our emotions—if they can only be heard. These are messages about the peace and contentment of knowing our finances are on track to meet our family's needs, and the unvarnished thrill of using our resources to touch the lives of others. The first step, though, is to establish or clarify a sense of direction, a purpose for our lives.

---

1   From the Foreword of *What Matters Most* by Jim Munchbach (Baxter Press, Friendswood, Texas, 2004), p. 9.

2   "Motivating Americans to Develop Constructive Financial Behaviors," by the National Endowment for Financial Education, 2004, p. 6.

Connecting the Dots

In relation to our finances, the path to peace and fulfillment is connecting our resources to what matters most to us. Many people, however, have never clearly articulated what really matters to them. When they do, incredible things happen.

Soon after I finished my training as a CERTIFIED FINANCIAL PLANNER™ professional, I met with a wealthy businessman. James grew up in a poor black neighborhood, and his family barely made ends meet day after day. As an adult, James was driven to make enough money so that his own family never experienced the fear of empty cupboards, and he made a lot of money. James had over a million dollars in his retirement account, and his half-million dollar home was completely paid for. Clearly, he had plenty of resources, but he lived with constant anxiety that he might not be able to provide enough for his family. No amount of money seemed to be enough to calm his anxious heart, so he drove himself day after day to make more sales.

Before James and his wife Sheila walked into my office, his goal had been to make as much money as possible to be sure his family wasn't in need. As we talked about his values, it became clear to him that his real purpose wasn't making a lot of money. It was stability and security for his family, and he wanted to feel a sense of peace about his role as their provider. We identified the goals that would fulfill his purpose, including the amounts of money required for his children's education, his daughter's wedding, and his retirement. We then outlined a plan so that all of these needs would be met. With the pressure to make more and more money off his back, he realized he would be able to spend far more time with his wife, his children, and his grandchildren. Before that moment, James had been so driven to make money, but now he had a clear vision for his life and the freedom to enjoy quality time with his family.

In only a few minutes, the expression on James' face changed entirely. Suddenly, he broke into a huge grin, and then he looked at his wife. They reached out to hold hands and looked into each other's eyes as if to say, "This is what we've been looking for." Their anxiety—and the tension it had created between them—had evaporated. They had come into my office confused and stressed, but they walked out with a profound sense of contentment and joy because they now looked forward to a future of rich, meaningful relationships. James was a new man with an achievable plan and the warm affirmation of his wife for being such a wonderful provider. I'd like to take a lot of credit for the change in James' life that day, but all I did was ask a few questions to clarify his goals and connect the dots between his resources and what mattered most to him.

Turning Point

Not long after Connie and I got married, we moved to Austin, Texas, and I got a job making more money than I ever dreamed of making. It wasn't that much, but to me, it seemed like a fortune! I was able to buy things Connie and I could enjoy, and for a while, it was wonderful. I sure didn't want to go into debt, but we spent every dime I made. Soon, though, the things I bought weren't enough to thrill me any longer. I wanted more. I thought I needed more. I hoped the things I was buying could fill up the hole in my heart, but when they didn't, I tried to cram more in there. But the hole just got bigger.

One day I realized that I had all I'd ever wanted—a wonderful wife, two beautiful sons, a good job, and lots of stuff—but I was miserable. My dream was fulfilled, but I felt emptier than ever. For a new thrill, I started smoking pot. That felt good for a while, but bad decisions followed bad decisions, and soon I was on the verge of losing Connie, my sons, my home, and my job. I'd like to say that I flushed

> *One day I realized that I had all I'd ever wanted—a wonderful wife, two beautiful sons, a good job, and lots of stuff—but I was miserable.*

my last dime bag down the toilet because of noble reasons, but that's not true. I flushed it because I realized it was costing me way too much money.

The answer, I became convinced, was to make even more money. I left my job and became an insurance agent. In that role, I interacted with hundreds of people, and I observed them carefully. Some were just as driven to make money as I was, and they felt just as empty. But surprisingly, many of the men and women who came to my office had a clear, compelling sense of direction for their lives, and they wanted to marshal every resource to fulfill their dreams. These people had learned one of life's most important lessons: We experience far more joy and fulfillment if we devote ourselves to others instead of spending our resources on our own pleasures.

I had read about these principles of "giving to live" in some Bible classes in college, but these clients were flesh and blood examples who were living those principles. I desperately wanted what they had, but I wasn't sure how to get it. One major turning point came when I signed up for the Financial Planning Association Residency Program. I went to the conference center a day early to spend time with some friends. That morning, I walked down to the restaurant to get some coffee, and I saw a man in his 50s coming out of the exercise room. He was the epitome of a handsome, fit, fabulously successful, got-it-all-together businessman. Instantly, I hated him. Our eyes met for a second, and we smiled and nodded to each other the way polite businessmen do. I hoped I would never see him again.

That afternoon, I walked in to the first meeting of the Residency Program, and there he was. He introduced himself, "Hello, my name is Rich." I hoped to avoid him as much as possible, but he was one of my mentors for the entire week. A few minutes later, all the mentors were asked to give thumbnail sketches of their business philosophies and how they serve their clients. When Rich's turn came, he told the group that he hoped to impart to us how much he treasures his clients. "My clients," he told us, "are more than account numbers and sources of commissions. They are people who entrust their hopes and dreams to me." He assured us that what matters most is not how much we know about investments, tax law, or retirement planning, and it's not how well we've perfected a particular set of sales techniques to get them to say "yes." It's about the people themselves.

Our calling, he said, is amazingly simple and immensely profound: to connect with people on the deepest level to earn their trust so they will share with us their dreams for their families and themselves. Instead of focusing on our *own* goal of getting them to buy a policy or invest some money so we can earn a commission, the focus shifts dramatically to *their* needs, *their* hopes, and *their* deepest desires. At the end of Rich's introduction, he spoke a sentence that has resonated in my heart since that moment: "When clients share their most heartfelt dreams with me, I consider that a sacred trust."

> *"When clients share their most heartfelt dreams with me, I consider that a sacred trust."*

Immediately, I realized: That's it! That's what I've been looking for: relationships based on trust that surface and enhance our most cherished dreams. That's what my clients wanted, but that's what I wanted, too. I had been completely absorbed in myself—my pleasure, my goals, my desires, my success, and my comfort. The circle of my life had been reduced to a dot. As a friend of mine says about his temptation to be preoccupied with himself, "I may not be much, but I'm all I think about." That was true of me—in spades! When I met with clients, I smiled and tried to look like I was genuinely interested in them, but I was thinking only about selling them products so I could make more money. And in my family, I demanded that they comply with my wishes all day, every day—or I pouted.

But Rich and the clients who had modeled a life of purpose were showing me that real life comes from looking beyond ourselves. I remembered that Jesus told his followers, "Give away your life; you'll find life given back, but not merely given back—given back with bonus and blessing. Giving, not getting, is the way. Generosity begets generosity" (Luke 6:38). I'd probably read or heard that passage dozens of times, but in Rich and my purpose-filled clients, I saw that it's true. Those who lived for a higher purpose than their own pleasure experienced the thrill of touching others' lives and the contentment of knowing their lives really count.

The change in my life has been wonderful . . . if a bit uneven. As I've become convinced that living for others brings the most joy in life, I've certainly experienced far greater contentment than ever before. Instead of demanding my way all the time with Connie and our kids (and my friends and co-workers and neighbors and anyone else in the universe), I really care about them. Instead of using Connie to meet my needs, I'm more concerned about her needs. Believe it or not, I'm learning to listen. Today, I see my defect of selfishness far more clearly than I did when I was submerged in it, and now I can more easily identify my selfish attitudes and actions so I can make choices to be more gracious and grateful. But make no mistake, I'm still in process, and I have a long way to go. I'm only on the first part of the path, but I'll tell you, even the beginning of the journey of caring for others is far better than the best day of rampant selfishness.

Everybody, All the Time

Many books about financial management focus almost exclusively on those who are deeply in debt. That's a significant audience, but the financial principles that bring fulfillment and adventure apply to all of us. Getting out of debt brings tremendous relief, but connecting our resources to what matters most produces a delicious blend of contentment and excitement. I believe that's what most of us long for.

The message of this book is for three distinct audiences: those in their 20s and 30s, who are just starting out and facing new responsibilities, those in their 40s and 50s, who are in their most productive years, and those in their 60s and above, who live with either great joy or regret because of past choices. Let me describe these audiences a bit more.

20s and 30s

I talk to a lot of young singles and couples who realize that their new responsibilities of work, marriage, children, and a home require them to learn to manage their money. Just out of college, many of them spent every penny they made on clothes, cars, ski trips, and anything else their friends were doing. But now, they want to get serious about their finances, and they're looking for some good advice.

40s and 50s

Many people in their 40s and 50s have settled into habits that are established—and maybe as hard as concrete. They've found a peer group they want to run with, and they have determined that they need to spend a certain amount of money to be accepted by them. In some cases, these habits include sound financial management, but often, these habits are monsters that need to be fed with more and more money. They're making a lot of money, but they're spending virtually all of it.

Others in this stage of life have a lot of money in home equity and in various investment and retirement accounts, but their finances leave them with a mysterious sense of emptiness. Beyond a comfortable retirement, they aren't sure what their money is for.

Some in this stage have only a modest amount of money in retirement accounts, but not nearly enough to provide the security their families need. Unless things change, they know they'll need to work until the day they die.

Over 60

Older people who come to my office seem to be full of either hope or despair. In most cases, their best income-producing years are over, and they look back on their decisions with either thankfulness or regret. Important lessons, however, are learned either way, so they still have a wonderful opportunity to impart wisdom to their children and grandchildren and leave a strong legacy.

VISION, INTENTION, AND MEANS: A VERY PERSONAL JOURNEY

In my own life and in the lives of countless people I've counseled, I've realized that change happens most readily and permanently if people have a clear picture of the future, a commitment to take steps of progress, and good handles on the steps they need to take. Elements of change, then, are *vision, intention,* and *means.* This book is structured with these three features in mind:

- The first three chapters focus on creating or clarifying our vision or our purpose in life. As we go though those chapters, some people may think, *Why is he taking so long to get to the nuts and bolts of budgeting and investing?* The reason is that these three chapters are essential to give us direction and motivation for the choices we make in the rest of the book.

- Chapter 4 takes us through "The Blueprint for Financial Success." The analysis we do in this step stimulates our intention to make the changes we need to make.

- The rest of the book, chapters 5 through 8, describes the principles and resources we can use to achieve the goals we set in the Blueprint.

Whatever you do, don't miss Chapter 6, "Small Steps, Big Payoffs." This chapter shows how seemingly insignificant choices in our daily lives make a huge difference in our financial security and opportunities down the road. For example, our choice of cars—choosing one with a $200 monthly payment instead of one with a $400 payment—can save us enough money to net over $1,000,000 when we're 65! Stay tuned. You don't want to miss that chapter.

I make no assumptions about what your purpose in life is or should be. The self-discovery you'll experience in these pages will clarify your life's purpose so you can connect everything you have and everything you do to what matters most to you. As I explained the content of the book to a friend of mine, he gave a half smile and shook his head. He told me, "Yeah, but most of the financial planning books that are written by Christians have the subtle—or not so subtle—intention of getting people to donate their money to the church's building fund. Is that your angle, too?"

No, I told him, that's not even on my radar. I hope people will think, dream, and plan so they accomplish something that gives them personal fulfillment. That "something" certainly involves their family's security, but it may also involve serving people in need through a host of organizations: Amnesty International, their church, Habitat for Humanity, or any of dozens of other groups that are trying to make a difference in people's lives.

As you've probably guessed, I'm a follower of Christ, so my own purpose in life is shaped to a large degree by my understanding of God's desires for me and every other person who follows him. The most powerful motivation I've known is the deep sense of gratitude that comes from experiencing the unconditional love and acceptance of Jesus Christ. Knowing his love and acceptance is by far the most incredible experience of my life. But in my work as a financial planner, I meet with Hindus, Buddhists, Muslims, agnostics, atheists, Jewish people, and others from every kind of religious stripe. Most of the principles of spending, saving, investing, and giving transcend all religions. We can apply them no matter what we believe about God. My faith, though, directs me to look beyond my own needs and try to help others.

My hope is that this book will give you a few "Aha!" moments when a light comes on and you realize a truth or an opportunity you'd missed before. Those moments inevitably lead to choices to move in a new direction (or go back to a previously beaten path). As you clarify your purpose and connect your resources to what you really value, I believe you'll feel relief and contentment, and you'll celebrate knowing your life counts for something much bigger than yourself.

> *In this book, I'm going to ask you to look at some aspects of your life—your heart and your money—as if you'd never seen them before.*

The process of connecting our resources to what matters most is exhilarating, but sometimes, it's not easy. In this book, I'm going to ask you to look at some aspects of your life—your heart and your money—as if you'd never seen them before. Have courage. It's worth the trouble!

At the end of this introduction and each chapter, you'll find some exercises and reflection questions. When I read books, I get far more out of them if I take a little more time to wrestle with the issues the author presents. These exercises and questions are designed to help you gain insights about your own motivations, perceptions, and goals. I hope you enjoy working through them. And by the way, they stimulate rich discussions with your family and friends, or in a class or small group. These sections are in two parts: "Think about it..." and "Going deeper." The first is designed to help you reflect on the connection between your purpose and your finances, and the second part specifically addresses Christian values for those of you who want to follow Christ in everything you do, including how you manage money.

THINK ABOUT IT...

1. Now that you know what this book is about, what do you want to happen in your life as a result of reading and studying it? (Consider your purpose in life, your closest relationships, your habits of managing money, and your future.)

Going deeper

1. Read Luke 6:38 again, and describe what that abundance might look like with regard to your relationship with God, your relationships with others, and your generosity with your time and other resources.

2. What is Jesus' promise to us in this passage?

1 | YOUR HEART'S DESIRE

"To look at something as though we had never seen it before requires great courage." —Henri Matisse, painter

I've met with hundreds of clients in every age group, and I'm convinced that good financial management doesn't begin with a pen and a checkbook. It starts with a good evaluation of what's in our hearts and minds. The choices we make with our money are a vivid portrait of our heart's desires and our thoughts about life. If we have a good grasp of these things, we will be able to keep the attitudes that bring fulfillment and toss away those that hinder us.

FOUR KINDS OF PEOPLE

In my discussions with people about financial planning, I've noticed that they seem to fall into one of four groups. These groups describe attitudes, not the amount of money they have. For instance, some people are "buried in debt." I know people who make $30,000 and fall into this category, but I also know people who make $1 million but spend $1.3 million each year. (Before long, being short $300,000 will catch up to you!) The amount of money isn't the determining factor. Instead, the attitude about life and money determines which kind of person we are. Here are the four kinds of people:

Buried in debt

Rick and Janice are both professionals in their 50s. He owns his own business, and she is an attorney. Together, they make over $250,000 a year, but they can't seem to make ends meet. Janice called me and scheduled an appointment. When they arrived at my office, the tension between them hung in the room like a storm cloud. They blamed each other for their predicament, and they were furious! I asked them some questions about their goals and dreams, but all they could think about was getting their debts paid off. That's a good start for people in their financial condition, so I asked them to show me the worksheet of their assets and liabilities so we could create a workable financial plan. It was like pulling teeth. They had a hard time even thinking of what they owned and what they owed, so I methodically asked questions to uncover the facts. In recent years, they had avoided this analysis like the plague because it was so painful to look at reality. It took a couple of sessions just to get most of the information we needed, but when we hit critical mass (and I realized I wasn't going to get any more from them), we started working on their plan.

Almost immediately, Rick told me that his car was old and he needed a new one. We talked about the reality of the numbers on the balance sheet we had been working on, and I suggested that he buy a good used car. That, he assured me, was out of the question. "I have an image to keep up," he insisted. "I need a brand new car . . . maybe a Lexus."

As soon as he said the word "Lexus," Janice blew up! She stood and yelled, "There you go again! All you care about is your 'image.' But you don't realize how you're ruining our lives!" She started walking out, and then she turned to me and said, "Jim, if you can't fix this, I'm going to file for divorce."

Some people have created their financial problems by their own poor choices, but others are buried in debt because they face difficulties that are beyond their control. I have a friend who was making about $40,000 a year and living modestly, but comfortably, with his wife and two children. He's a very responsible provider for his family, and he was slowly and steadily building his retirement fund. His wife got pregnant with twins, and he began making adjustments to make sure he had enough money for the delivery and the first years of the children's lives. But as the delivery date approached, the doctor told them there were complications. One of the twins had a heart defect and may not live to term. A month later, the children were born prematurely. One was healthy, but the other had severe heart problems. She was rushed to pediatric ICU, and surgery was scheduled as soon as possible. Two weeks after the surgery, the little girl died. The half-million-dollar bill the hospital sent them compounded the family's sadness. Through many negotiations, the hospital agreed to accept a fraction of the bill, but even the lower amount swamped the grieving parents. It took years, but they finally paid off these bills.

Many of those who are buried in debt, however, are like Rick and Janice, who have a "Santa Claus mentality." For some reason, they believe that somebody, somewhere will magically come through for them whenever they have a need. They have convinced themselves that they are going to win the lottery, that their boss will give them a huge bonus, or that Aunt Phoebe will die and leave all of her estate to them instead of her own children. With that assurance, they keep spending money like there's no tomorrow. A friend of mine has observed people like this, and he says they get a kind of "high" from spending. The euphoria they experience from buying new stuff fuels their desire to do it again and again. But like an addiction, no matter how much they get, it's never enough.

> *The euphoria they experience from buying new stuff fuels their desire to do it again and again. But like an addiction, no matter how much they get, it's never enough.*

Most people who are buried in debt suffer under atrocious credit card interest rates. In a letter to a personal finance columnist, a man admitted he owed $12,000 in unsecured debt, and he was paying 29.99 percent. He said that he always tried to pay a little more than the minimum, "but the balance never goes down." The writer responded with the discouraging news that at his current rate of payments, it would take more than 30 years to pay off his debt—if he didn't buy anything else in those 30 years.[3]

A generation ago, bank deregulation set off a race to sign up as many customers as possible, with the limits on interest rates significantly raised. Not surprisingly, many customers enjoyed the easy money credit cards afford, but they were shocked to find that the initial, reasonable interest rate skyrocketed when they were late with a payment. Getting those rates reduced is almost impossible. If they had read the fine print, they'd know that the credit card companies would charge those exorbitant rates.

Banks thrive on borrowers who are up to their eyeballs in credit card debt, but they make far less on the rest of us. In their article on this personal financial crisis, Joe Lee and Thomas Parrish explain: "In today's strange alternative universe of credit card banks, the term 'deadbeat' refers not to the improvident borrower but to the solid citizen who prides himself on paying off his balance every month. . . . What these lenders seek are 'revolvers' . . . who are likely to pay little more than the monthly minimum—and who eventually find themselves in thrall to mushrooming interest payments, abundantly garnished with late fees."

We need to realize that banks' ads may be attractive, but they don't have our best interests at heart. Their corporate commitment to their shareholders is to make as much money as possible. They offer tantalizing promises of low interest rates to hook people, and then they hope those people will miss payments so the bank can raise their rates. And it's perfectly legal.

For people who are buried in debt, thinking patterns tend to the extremes. Many, like Rick and Janice, refuse to even think about the negative consequences of their choices. They just drift along month to month hoping nobody will notice their mounting pile of unpaid bills. But then, when the collection agency sends a demand letter, panic replaces denial. For weeks or months, their minds are consumed day and night with fearful nightmares about a bleak future

---

[3] From the article, "Dazed and in debt in the credit card maze," by Joe Lee and Thomas Parrish, *The Houston Chronicle*, January 21, 2007.

alternating with hopeful daydreams about magically getting bailed out. ("I hear Aunt Phoebe isn't feeling too well!")

Barely above water

Bob and Rachel, both in their late 20s, just got married. It was a beautiful wedding, and now the happy couple is off to make a life of their own. Both of them have good jobs, but since they graduated from college, they spent virtually every penny they made. Sometimes they saved money for a special vacation, like the trip to Cancun, but they never had any cushion in their finances. They didn't feel euphoric when they spent money, but they didn't have a clear vision for their future, either. All they cared about was staying out of debt and having some cash to buy some fun stuff if they could afford it. That philosophy of financial life seemed fine to them—until the transmission fell out of Rachel's car, and they received a bill for over $2000.

People who are satisfied to be barely above water live "one paycheck from disaster," and they almost never see it coming. Often, these are young singles and couples who haven't experienced health problems, and they haven't owned a home so they haven't had to pay for major repairs. But those of us who have struggled with these things could have told them that significant surprises are a part of life. As an insurance professional, I've seen people hit with all kinds of unexpected problems, such as car accidents, hurricanes, floods, fires, medical bills, and traffic tickets. As we get a little older, we may face the death of a loved one who failed to provide enough money in his estate for a decent funeral. Today, a big expense many of us face is taking care of our aging parents. People who live barely above water aren't prepared for any of these surprises. Even relatively minor setbacks, like the $2000 car repair, can devastate their financial world, and consequently, cause immense strain on the relationships they value.

Of course, I know several individuals and couples who make far more money than Bob and Rachel, but their goal is to enjoy as much pleasure and comfort as possible today. As long as they don't go into debt (for too long, at least), they feel like they're winning the game. They're far more responsible than those who are buried in debt, and they aren't in denial about their financial situations, but they lack a compelling purpose outside their own wants that could give them direction and fulfillment.

Young adults can find themselves at the painful juncture of incredibly high expectations and painful reality. Most of them grew up enjoying a lifestyle full of perks. Even in homes with modest incomes, a "normal" lifestyle included a cell phone, an Xbox or Game Boy, the latest MP3 player, a lightning-fast computer, and of course, the latest fashions and plenty of money for movies, trips, and other kinds of entertainment. Their experience with amenities and wealth created the expectation that they'd have even more when they graduated and went out on their own. Psychologist Jean Twenge, a professor at San Diego State University, wrote the insightful book, *Generation Me: Why Today's Young Americans Are More Confident, Assertive, Entitled—and More Miserable Than Ever Before.* She notes, "There are a lot of young people hitting 25 who are making, say $35,000 a year, who expected they'd be millionaires or at least making six figures."[4] Many of these young adults spend every penny they make to maintain the lifestyle they've enjoyed, and they're financially barely above water. Almost any unexpected expense sends them over the brink into debt. I know some young adults who experienced the pain of unfulfilled expectations. Some became disillusioned and bitter, but many of them used their disappointment as a steppingstone for change.

Not long ago, I came across a word that captures the disappointment that results from unrealistic expectations. Weltschmerz (pronounced velt-shmerts) is a German word that means, "Mental depression or apathy caused by comparison of the actual state of the

---

[4] Quoted in *The Houston Chronicle*, "A generation obsessed with having more stuff," by Martha Irvine, January 23, 2007.

world with an ideal state." And as we all know, comparison kills. Realistic expectations, however, combat all the distorted thinking and the promises of advertising, and we can then make good choices based on truth and live with a profound sense of peace.

Sadly, when I talk to people who are barely above water about developing a financial plan, many of them tell me, "Oh, I don't need that. What good would it do? I don't have any extra money." That's precisely the reason they need one.

Bucks in the bank, but still worried

In my own story, when I realized that living barely above water and buying lots of stuff didn't provide real fulfillment, I changed course. Unfortunately, my solution was only to make a lot more money, not to find true purpose that could guide every aspect of my life, including my finances. When I became an insurance agent, I was determined to make as much money as possible. During that period of my life, I was the poster child for this category: I had bucks in the bank, but I always worried that I wouldn't have enough.

Many of my clients and friends fall into this category. For some reason, they have an almost insatiable appetite for *more*. They realize there's a lot of money out there just waiting for someone to come along with a good product or service and a little marketing savvy. Millions of dollars are waiting for them, and they're determined to gather all they can. They're willing to do *whatever it takes* to get what they want, and many of them sacrifice everything—family, health, hobbies, and even a measure of sanity—in the pursuit of a fatter bank statement. But it's never enough.

> *"What is it that you really want? What's missing that you long for?"*

I talked with a client who is fabulously wealthy, and we discussed his relentless chase for more money. After a while, I asked him, "What is it that you really want? What's missing that you long for?"

He looked at me as if to say, *Jim, that's a dumb question. Don't you know the answer already?* Then he said simply, "Peace."

Of course, not everybody in this category has great wealth. Most of them have a nice retirement fund through their company or their own investments, and they actually have a reasonable amount of money to do the things they enjoy. The issue with these people isn't the number at the bottom of their balance sheet. It's the fact that their significant resources aren't directed by a strong sense of purpose. Without that benchmark, no amount of money ever seems to be enough to fill the hole in their hearts.

Full of purpose and contentment

I have a few friends who are attentive about their financial health, but they don't worry about it. They read and learn about investments, and they ask good questions to get the information they need. They use that information and a strong set of values to shape their choices about spending, investing, and giving wisely. These people have established their sense of purpose in life, and they measure every decision according to that purpose. They have learned that the secret of life is to live for a cause that's much bigger than themselves, and they are terrific examples for their families, their friends, and everyone who knows them. They live with a strong sense of thankfulness that combats worry, pride, and consumerism.

Many years ago, a group of Christians exemplified this lifestyle of wisdom, prudence, and generosity. They were the Puritans. Today, most of us think of them as rigid and stoic, but that's not the case at all. In my study of their lifestyle, I've been inspired by the depth of their commitment to a transcendent purpose and their sheer, unmitigated joy in seeing God use them to touch others' lives. That's really attractive to me! They believed that everything they owned was a gift from God, and this perspective stimulated them to be responsible to use those gifts effectively and to celebrate God's goodness to them. They had a terrific balance of enjoying their resources and being wise financial managers who shrewdly invested to make more money. This combination of characteristics, coupled with their compassion for people in need, enabled them to be very generous.

I see a few people around me today who have those same perspectives, and I want to spend as much time with them as possible. They are committed to excellence, but they aren't driven by an inordinate, insatiable desire to have more money, possessions, comfort, and pleasure. When they go home at the end of the day, they can rest because their hearts and minds are at peace. They struggle with problems that we all face, but they can address those things from a personal history of wisdom, good communication with their spouse and kids, and trust that God is at work in the good times and bad.

LIES WE BELIEVE

We live in the wealthiest society the world has ever known. Even those at the bottom of the economic ladder enjoy technology (televisions and cell phones) and transportation (cars or mass transit) that was unthinkable even to the super rich a few generations ago. Why, then, are so many people unhappy with what they have? Why do we have such a powerful desire to have more?

Though it certainly isn't the only cause for our discontent, advertising has had a powerful impact on our expectations. The purpose of advertising is to create discontent. In his book, *The Technological Society*, French cultural analyst Jacques Ellul observed, "One of the great designs of advertising is to create needs; but this is possible only if these needs correspond to an ideal of life that man accepts. The way of life offered by advertising is all the more compelling in that it corresponds to certain easy and simple tendencies of man and refers to a world in which there are no spiritual values to form and inform life. When men feel and respond to the needs advertising creates, they are adhering to its ideal of life. The human tendencies upon which advertising like this is based may be strikingly simpleminded, but they nonetheless represent pretty much the level of our modern life. Advertising offers us the ideal we have always wanted (and that ideal is certainly not a heroic way of life)."[5]

Ellul's insights are brilliant and piercing. The "ideal" life depicted in modern advertising promises to fulfill our expectations of

---

5 jan.ucc.nau.edu/~jsa3/hum355/readings/ellul.htm

wealth, ease, happiness, and entertainment. In stark contrast, the "heroic" life is one of honor, duty, sacrifice, and joyful service to others. Why do we focus so much on acquiring more stuff? Dale Carnegie stated succinctly, "We are creatures of emotion, bristling with prejudice and motivated by pride and vanity." Selfishness crowds out heroism.

> *In stark contrast, the "heroic" life is one of honor, duty, sacrifice, and joyful service to others.*

In an interview with Luci Shaw for Radix magazine, Dallas Willard, author of *The Divine Conspiracy*, reflected on the impact of rampant consumption in our culture: "We are designed to be creators, initiators, not just receivers. Yet the whole model, the consumerist model of the human being, is to make us passive, and to make us complainers and whiners, because we're not being given what we need. We cook up a 'right' to that and then we say we've been deprived of our rights. We see this in our churches, which pander to consumers. They say, 'Come and consume the services we offer, and we guarantee you a wonderful time. You'll go out of the church door feeling good.' "[6]

The same truth is stated by a very different source. In their hit song, "The Grand Illusion," the rock group Styx observes that our culture has an insatiable appetite for more and more stuff without every stopping to reflect on the purpose of life. They sing, "Someday soon we'll stop to ponder what on Earth's this spell we're under. We made the grade and still we wonder who the hell we are."[7]

Let me be quick to say that I'm not accusing any individual. Instead, these observations are an indictment of our entire culture. These characteristics are pervasive, to some degree affecting every one of us. The deceptive messages that we need—and, in fact, *deserve*—more and more possessions and pleasure are the air

---

[6] "Spiritual Disciplines in a Postmodern World," Luci Shaw with Dallas Willard, Radix, Vol. 27, No. 2. Online at www.dwillard.org/articles/artview.asp?artid=56

[7] "The Grand Illusion," The Greatest Hits, Styx, 1995.

we breathe each day. And the impact is devastating to our values, dreams, and purposes. Daniel Yankelovich, author of the insightful book *New Rules,* observes that in only the past 50 years, our culture has shifted from self-sacrifice to self-indulgence. The generation that willingly gave their lives to defeat totalitarianism in Germany and Japan would hardly recognize us today. It's been a quick slide.

Pulling Weeds

One of Jesus' parables describes several different responses to truth, but for our purposes, we'll focus on two of the responses. In "The Parable of the Soils," Jesus said that truth falls on the ground, and if there's enough soil, light, and moisture, the seed sprouts. One of the soils, however, has a problem: weeds. Jesus said, "And the seed that fell in the weeds—well, these are the ones who hear, but then the seed is crowded out and nothing comes of it as they go about their lives worrying about tomorrow, making money, and having fun" (Luke 8:14). The first three kinds of people we've examined in this chapter—those who are buried in debt, those who are barely above water, and those who have money but are still worried—all have had their spiritual vitality choked out by the weeds of worry, the empty promises that having more money will bring true fulfillment, and the tragedy of wasting our resources on things that don't really matter.

Another type of soil in Jesus' parable corresponds to the fourth kind of person in our study. About these people, Jesus said, "But the seed in the good earth—these are the good-hearts who seize the Word and hold on no matter what, sticking with it until there's a harvest" (Luke 8:15). Another translation says that these people produce an enormous harvest, 30, 60, or 100 times as much as they started with. But I don't think Jesus was talking only about money. He was talking about every aspect of our lives: our relationships with family and friends, our work, our care for those who are in need, as well as our choices about money.

Some of us might be tempted to think that people in the productive soil have it made, that they never struggle with any problems. But that's not the case. They're just good weed pullers. They listen to the same messages and experience the same temptations as the rest of us, but they have a strong sense of purpose, and that gives them clarity in their choices.

Or we might think that these folks have to just grit their teeth and do the right thing even though they don't really want to. To be sure, sometimes doing the right thing is hard, but the focus for these people is the sheer thrill of seeing their lives count for something far bigger than themselves. Instead of the circle of their lives being reduced to a dot, it's expanded to touch countless others. No, they don't just grit their teeth and make a good decision. They think, *I can't believe God is so good to me that he lets me be involved in the greatest adventure the universe has ever known: changing lives!*

> *The focus for these people is the sheer thrill of seeing their lives count for something far bigger than themselves.*

At another time and place, Jesus described two messages and the outcome of listening to those messages. One is communicated by a "thief," someone whose goal is only to take from us, not to build value into our lives. The other message is Jesus' message of life to us. He said, "A thief is only there to steal and kill and destroy. I came so they can have real and eternal life, more and better life than they ever dreamed of" (John 10:10). As I've interacted with clients and friends (and looked in the mirror), I've seen a stark contrast in the expressions on people's faces. Those who listen to the deceptive messages (that we deserve all the possessions and pleasures we can grab) may experience delight for a season, but they are never truly satisfied. In contrast, those who listen to the message that the greatest fulfillment comes when we give our lives away experience the thrill of being fully alive. That's what I want, and it's my guess that it's what you want, too.

GET A GYROSCOPE

You and I live all day, every day in the culture of self-indulgence. If we're aware of it, we can do something about it. From my own experience, I've learned that living a life without a transcendent purpose is a dead end street. Santa Claus isn't going to bail us out, and there's much more to life than barely making it each month or living in fear that no amount of money is enough.

For most of us, living a life of purpose will require some adjustments. The question is: Is it worth it? For me, the answer is emphatically "yes!" I'm still tempted by those messages that I deserve the newest this or the best that, but I'm far more aware of those messages today, so I can more clearly see the choices. Over the past decade, I've been reorienting my life according to the purposes that challenge me and fill my heart with gratitude. As I've looked beyond my own selfish needs and tried to meet some of the needs of those around me, I've seen God use me to touch a few lives—and that both humbles me and thrills me. Sure, I could work harder and make more money, but I've gradually become deeply convinced that there are things more important than a little more money.

In his book, *The Call,* author Os Guinness described the powerful, clear sense of purpose in the lives of the Puritans as an internal gyroscope that kept them on track no matter what was going on around them. That's what my purpose is becoming for me.

Someday, each of us will receive a report card of our attitudes and behaviors. You and I have been given great wealth in time, resources, and abilities. Jesus once remarked, "Great gifts mean great responsibilities; greater gifts, greater responsibilities!" (Luke12:48) If we squander those great gifts on meaningless things, we'll regret it now, and we'll regret it even more when the report card comes out.

A good grade isn't based on not having any weeds. No, we get a good grade because we had the perception to see the weeds of worry and selfishness, and we mustered the courage to pull them whenever we saw them. I want to be a good weed puller.

THINK ABOUT IT...

1. On any list of the top 10 stresses in people's lives, where does money rank for most of us? What does this stress look like?

2. Think about the four types of people described in this chapter: What are the thought patterns that keep people in each of these categories?
   —Buried in debt

   —Barely above water

   —Bucks in the bank, but still worried

   —Full of purpose and contentment

   How are family relationships affected by these thoughts, attitudes, and choices in each category?

3. Look at these descriptions of the four types of money managers, and circle the specific ones in any category that closely fit your experience:

—Buried in debt
- You often wonder how the bills will get paid.
- You experience tension with family members about spending.
- You get a little high from buying something you want, then depressed when the bill comes due.
- You don't want to even think about money.

—Barely above water
- You would have difficulty paying an unexpected bill of $2000.
- You often look at your bank statement to see if you have enough money to pay for things.
- You experience tension with family members about spending.
- You love Christmas, but paying bills in January is a stretch.

—Bucks in the bank, but still worried
- You don't think you ever have enough money so you can relax.
- You are driven to earn more.
- You experience tension with family members about spending.
- You often check your fund balances.

—Full of purpose and contentment
- You are thoughtful and responsible in financial planning.
- You stick to the plan and avoid frivolous spending.
- Your purpose is a gyroscope that gives you stability and direction.
- You are thrilled that your life really counts.

Based on your answers, which one best characterizes you as a money manager? Explain your answer.

4. Think of the pervasive nature of advertising, and look back at the quotes in this chapter about advertising and consumerism. As best you can, describe the impact of advertising on your choices. How might your choices be different if you weren't exposed to the powerful effects of advertising?

5. What are some ways a strong sense of purpose could be a gyroscope in your life? What difference would it make?

Going deeper

1. Read Luke 8:14-15. Give several examples of how these weeds choke out our spiritual vitality.

    —Worrying that we won't have enough:

    —The deceitfulness of wealth:

    —The desire to fill our lives with pleasure:

2. Which weed threatens to choke out your spiritual vitality? Explain your answer.

3. Think of the fourth soil and those who are filled with purpose and contentment. What does it mean to be a good weed puller?

4. What would that look like in your life today?

2 | First Memories about Money

"Happiness is nothing more than good health and a bad memory."
—Albert Schweitzer

My uncle Hank is a wonderful, but complicated, man. He is one of the most generous, gracious people I've ever known, but when it comes to spending money on himself, he can be incredibly tight. A couple of years ago, he told me perhaps his most powerful childhood memory. He grew up on a small farm, and his dad raised cattle. The only cash Hank's dad earned was from the sale of calves each year. Uncle Hank told me that in one of those bleak years, his father handed all of his calves to a broker who was to sell them and bring him the profits. The broker, though, was a crook, who ran off with the money. Hank told me, "I came in the house that day, and my father was sitting at the table crying. I'd never seen my dad cry before. Those calves represented our family's income for the whole year."

As we continued to talk about that traumatic moment, Uncle Hank explained that seeing his dad cry filled him with fear that someday, somehow he, too, wouldn't have enough money for his family. That fear drove him to be shrewd in handling money. He became a very successful businessman and investor, but his fear also made him extremely reluctant to spend money. He has always been very generous with his family, but extremely frugal about spending money on himself. Those traits sound like great strengths—and they are in most cases—but Uncle Hank's fear produced tension that could keep him from celebrating his wealth and his life. In moderation, being frugal is a wonderful strength, but some people cling to their money because they are motivated by fear or pride. Money is meant to accomplish good and noble purposes, so frugality only has meaning if it channels our money to efficiently use our resources to fulfill our life's purposes.

Connecting the Dots

When I meet with people, I often ask them a couple of questions: "What are some of your early memories about money?" and "What are some ways those experiences affect your attitudes and choices about money today?" I've been amazed at some of the stories people have told me, and I've also been amazed at their insights about the life-changing impact of these experiences. Let me share a few with you.

- Kim told me that when she was about five years old, her aunt suggested that she save some of her 25-cent allowance each week to buy something she really wanted. Instantly, she knew exactly what that would be: a ballerina watch! She had seen it at a store for $3.25. Kim saved her money every week, and in exactly thirteen weeks, she and her aunt marched into the store to buy the watch. Kim reflected, "To this day, I've always realized that to get something I really want, I have to be disciplined to save for it. That's a lesson I learned from my aunt and a pretty pink ballerina watch."

- Taylor is only 25, but he learned valuable lessons from his first two jobs. His first one was a minimum wage job at a T-shirt store at the mall. He worked after school and on Saturdays, and he spent most of his time folding shirts and looking for something to fill his time. He soon realized that jobs like that are incredibly boring, and some of his friends were making a lot more money waiting tables at local restaurants. Taylor isn't a quitter, so he stayed at the shop as long as he could stand it, but after a year, he applied for a job at a steak restaurant. Instead of being bored, he now came home frazzled because the complexity of orders, the pace, and the need to interact amiably with customers stressed him out. But he was making far more money from tips than he made at the mall, and that kept him motivated. At the store in the mall, Taylor learned that minimum wage jobs may not require much of you, but they don't reward you much, either. As a waiter, he found out that hard work pays off, and that generosity is one of the highest virtues. He has graduated from college and is making a good living in a job he loves. Even today, when he goes out to eat with his dad, he checks to be sure his father leaves a sizeable tip. That's important to Taylor.

> *As a waiter, he found out that hard work pays off, and that generosity is one of the highest virtues.*

- Peter didn't have any trouble remembering an important event about money from his childhood. He told me that his father made a lot of money in the furniture business—so much money that he bought diamonds and furs for Peter's mom. But when Peter was about nine, suddenly the market changed and the store went out of business. He remembered, "All of a sudden, we went from riches to wondering if we were going to eat. It was awful. I didn't really know what was going on. All I knew was that my mother was really upset. One day, she boxed up a lot of her nice clothes, and we took them to a place downtown. After we got there, I realized she was selling her nicest clothes to get some money to buy food. I remember that moment like it was ten minutes ago. We hauled the boxes into the store. A lady looked through them and then offered my mother $2. Mom was furious! The look on her face has been embedded in my mind all these years. On that day, I realized that our family wasn't safe any more—that I wasn't safe any more—and that I had to be sure not to ever be out of money. From that moment until today, I've been very frugal and very private about my finances."

- Janice told me about a friend who was repeatedly abused sexually by her father. The day after each encounter, her father bought her something nice to buy her silence. Today, years later, whenever she's anxious, Janice's friend spends money on herself so she'll feel better. The connection between the pain of abuse and gifts from her dad is still riveted on her soul and her spending habits. The trail of her maxed-out credit cards leads directly back to those days when her father tried to put salve on her pain and his guilt by buying her nice things.

- My wife Connie remembers that when she got her first job at Catfish Parlor when she was in high school, she had her eye on some fine leather boots that came almost up to her knees. At the time, they were very stylish, but they were also very expensive. She realized she would have to save every penny she made for an entire month to pay for them. And that's exactly what she did. She told me, "I was so sure those boots would really make me happy, and they did—for about three weeks. But then they went out of style and they weren't important to me any more."

   I asked, "Has that experience affected how you spend and save today?"

   "You know it has," she laughed. "I'm really careful about the way I spend money. I don't ever again want to feel like I've wasted hard-earned money on things that don't last, or worse, on things that become worthless so quickly."

- My first memory about money occurred when I was about five years old. My father had just been discharged from the military, and we were very poor, living in a trailer park. One day, I went with my mother to check the mail. When the box was empty, I could tell she was really sad and anxious. I realized she was looking for a letter with some money in it. After she went back to the trailer, I went to check all the other mailboxes until I found some mail to bring back to her. I wasn't the most observant five-year-old—I thought *all* mail included some money. (I hadn't gone to law school, so I didn't know I'd committed a federal offense!) The manager caught me, and he wasn't too happy about it! That day, I learned that money has the power to make people happy or sad, and I wanted to do anything to make my mother happy.

- Another experience shaped my drive to make money. When I was ten or eleven, I had a paper route with the Detroit Free Press. The newspaper had a contest: Whoever got the most new subscriptions would win a huge case of assorted candy (M&M's, Reese's Peanut Butter Cups, Snickers, Hershey Bars, etc.). I was motivated! I gave up kickball, family picnics, and everything I enjoyed so I could devote every waking hour to sell the Detroit Free Press. I wanted the prize, so I went from house to house, apartment to apartment, and trailer to trailer to talk to people. I was tenacious, and I wouldn't take "no" for an answer. In a few weeks, the results of the contest were announced, and I had won first prize. All my friends came to my room to see the stack of goodies and select their favorite candy bar.

That experience may not seem like a big deal. After all, it was only a case of candy. But it demonstrated to me that if I was driven enough, I could get anything I wanted. It would take me years (and a lot of pain) to realize that being driven to achieve financial success might cause me to miss out on some far more important treasures in life (like a great game of kickball). Those two events—looking for money in other people's mail when I was five and the intense drive to succeed in getting new subscribers for the Detroit Free Press—are connected. I probably wouldn't have had the emotional intensity about being successful if I hadn't been propelled by the fear of not having enough.

Some of us can easily think of our "first memories" when we were very young, but others more easily recall the delight of getting their first paycheck from their first job in high school or the finances related to some other important event in their lives. Most of us can remember several events pertaining to money that shaped our lives. The important issue is to reflect on events that are important enough for us to remember them. Each of these is probably

> *Most of us can remember several events pertaining to money that shaped our lives.*

significant in more ways than we first imagine.

The questions I ask my clients are helpful to everybody, but they may be especially helpful to those who are buried in debt or barely above water. Sometimes when I talk about finances (and specifically spending habits) to people in these groups, some of them shake their heads and tell me, "I don't know why in the world I do some of the things I do. Sometimes I buy things even though I know I can't afford them. It just doesn't make sense." But actually, if we connect the dots of our present attitudes and behaviors to important moments in our past, it might make perfect sense! With those insights, we more clearly see our choices so we can make better decisions.

The Impact of Parents

Not surprisingly, parents shape our perceptions about life and money to a large degree. I've thought about the hundreds of people I've counseled about their finances, and I can say that every person who had parents who were good models in handling finances has a mature, responsible view of money and far less anxiety than the rest of us.

A friend of mine is in her late 20s. She told me about a time when she was about six, and she and her dad were at a grocery store picking up a few things for dinner. As they came around a corner, her dad spotted a folded $50 bill on the floor. He picked it up and told her, "Come on. We're going to take this to the Customer Service Desk." When they got there, her dad only told the clerk that he had found something valuable. When the clerk asked what it was, her dad replied, "Here's my name and number. If somebody can describe it, I'll give it to him." The little girl wasn't sure why her dad wouldn't tell the guy what they'd found. A few minutes later, she and her dad heard his name called on the intercom. They went to the Customer Service Desk, and a distraught lady said, "I lost a $50 bill. Is that what you found?"

Her dad replied, "It sure is. Here you go." And he gave her the bill. The now-grown daughter recalls that by his example, her father taught her two valuable lessons: to have integrity, but not to trust other people too much.

Parents can model responsibility, generosity, and wisdom in managing risks. Imparting these traits is the goal of attentive parents. But even painful memories of our parents' poor example can have a powerfully positive impact on us. Uncle Hank's memory of the broker scamming his father and his father's grief taught him that the lack of money and trusting the wrong people devastate a family. That pain drove Uncle Hank to be a shrewd investor, to do plenty of research before he writes a check, and to be sure he provides for his own family.

Those who feel wounded by their parents can respond in a number of ways:

- Like Uncle Hank, their resolve can drive them to think clearly and act responsibly.

- They may become irresponsible, living for today without clear direction for their futures.

- They may look for someone else to bail them out when they get into financial trouble instead of being disciplined and making good decisions.

- They may become passive, paralyzed by indecision, feeling overwhelmed by the threat of making the wrong choice.

- They may become impulsive, taking big risks that sometimes hit it big, but often fail miserably. They keep looking, though, for the next big deal that will solve all their problems.

- They may become rigid, fearful of losing control of their finances and their lives.

Some of us don't have painful memories of our parents, but damage was done because our parents were too indulgent. They spoiled us. I've known some people who exhibited the traits I've identified as associated with painful pasts, but their parents were too attentive, too involved, and too generous. They failed to teach their kids about wisdom and responsibility, so the kids developed "learned helplessness," a passivity that expects others to take care of them. Unless there's a physical or mental disability, young people need to grow up and assume responsibility for their lives. Today, we see a lot of young people (mostly men) who are moving back with their parents after graduating from college and trying life in the business world for a few years. Many of them lack confidence, and they want to go back to a place where others will make hard decisions for them. That's a sad condition—not because they've chosen to live with their parents, but because their parents probably haven't given them the two things all children need, roots and wings, to enable them to be successful, independent adults.

One of the most damaging effects of parents' failure to impart financial wisdom is the inability to connect *cause* and *effect*. Many people simply believe that "things will work out" without any hint of discipline on their part. This "magical thinking" surfaces in a number of ways, including:

- The percentage of consumer debt to personal income has doubled in the past decade. Many people buy without thinking about having to pay off the debt.

- When young people receive too much money from their parents, they don't learn discipline and self-control, and they look for "easy money" wherever they can find it. Some gamble, looking for the big win, some borrow from friends, and some become dependent on credit. As their debts mount, they redouble their gamble, beg more intensely for handouts from friends, or search for another credit card.

> *When young people receive too much money from their parents, they don't learn discipline and self-control*

- The annual Retirement Confidence Survey reports that almost half of the people who haven't saved a single dime for retirement are "somewhat confident" they will have a comfortable retirement. They really believe that somebody, somehow, sometime will come through for them, even though they haven't done a single thing about their future.[8]

- Some young people have a pitiful (or nonexistent) work ethic. Since their parents have given them everything they've ever wanted, they don't have drive, determination, and discipline. I know a young man who is 28, but his parents still treat him like he's in grade school. He went to college as long as he could, but eventually, his grades were so bad that he couldn't find a school that would take him. He lives with some friends, but he depends on his parents to give him money for gas, groceries, rent, and everything else. His mother recently paid off his second fine for DWI, but she's keeping it a secret from his dad. Instead of being grateful for her generosity, he demands even more.

Why don't more parents impart wisdom and responsibility about money to their kids? I think there are five primary reasons:

- Some parents have been consumed with earning more money. They've neglected their families, and they *feel guilty*. They try to absolve their guilt by buying their kids' affection. This teaches the kids they can have anything they want, and it stifles their sense of responsibility.

- Some of them are *ashamed* of how they handle their finances, and they simply don't want to talk about an area that causes them so much pain and anxiety.

- On the other hand, some feel tremendous *pride* in their success. Their attitude is, "I'm rich, and it's none of your business, kid. It's mine, and I'm going to enjoy it myself."

- But many parents fail to be good examples for their kids simply because they are *replicating the poor model* of their own parents.

---

8 "Motivating Americans to Develop Constructive Financial Behaviors," by the National Endowment for Financial Education, 2004, p. 7.

They haven't seen what good parents do to train their kids in money matters, and they haven't developed these skills on their own.

- Some of us fail to teach our kids important lessons because we want *to protect them from pain*. On the morning before Super Bowl XL, Colts Head Coach Tony Dungy was the featured speaker at a breakfast in Detroit. The room fell silent as Dungy shared stories about his three sons, including James, his oldest son, who tragically died three days before Christmas only weeks before. Dungy spoke eloquently about lessons he learned from his painful experience. He then spoke of his middle son, Eric, who shares his competitiveness, and he described his youngest son, Jordan, who has a rare congenital condition that prevents him from feeling pain. "He feels things, but he doesn't get the sensation of pain," Dungy explained. "That sounds like it's good, but I promise you it's not. We've learned a lot about pain in the five years we've had Jordan. We've learned some hurts are really necessary for kids. Pain is necessary for kids to find out the difference between what's good and what's harmful. Pain sometimes lets us know we have a condition that needs to be healed. Pain inside sometimes lets us know that spiritually we're not quite right, and we need to be healed." For Tony Dungy and the rest of us, protecting our children from pain can prevent them from learning crucial lessons about life, relationships, and money.

I hope your parents imparted wisdom and responsibility to you. If they did, call them to thank them. If they didn't, don't despair. Wounds can be some of our greatest teachers, and in fact, resolving a painful past often gives people a deeper grasp of wisdom and purpose than they could get in any other way. I know some courageous people who have wrestled with the pain of abuse or neglect, found forgiveness and hope, and now are making responsible choices that thrill them and help others. In fact, some of the most wonderful models I know are single moms who realize it's now up to them to impart wisdom and responsibility to their children. And they're doing it.

Without the support of a husband and the role model of the children's father, the task is difficult, but they turn every obstacle and heartache into opportunities to teach life-changing lessons. Their kids may not realize how special their moms are, but their lives will be far better because of their mother's courage.

Opposites Attract . . . and Sometimes Explode!

We not only bring our memories of money into our own adulthoods; our spouses bring theirs, too. Psychologists tell us that most of us were attracted to characteristics in our mates that are opposite of ours, but they also tell us that, in marriage counseling, the four major areas of conflict are money, sex, children, and in-laws. Different perceptions about money can cause some of the biggest explosions in marriage.

My friend Kyle grew up in a strong, healthy home. His dad taught him the value of working hard and managing money. A few years ago, Kyle fell in love with Stephanie, but

"Let me see if I can understand where you're coming from."

soon after they got back from the honeymoon, sparks started flying. Stephanie's parents were wealthy, and they gave her everything she wanted. She never had to work, and she never kept track of the money she spent. You can imagine the friction in her relationship with Kyle! He came home each day having labored to provide for them, and he carefully managed his income. But Stephanie spent their money faster than he could earn it. When he tried to talk to her about it, she often exploded, "You don't love me! If you did, you wouldn't pressure me about the things I want to buy."

When I graduated from college and got a job as a mechanic, Connie and I had some of our most intense arguments over money. Out of every paycheck, I spent about $200 on new tools. She thought I was crazy to spend that much money, but I explained that the tools were crucial to my career. Even though I wasn't making much money, I put a little of our income in savings each pay period. She shook her head and told me, "We can't afford that!" I also bought a life insurance policy that had guaranteed cash value, but Connie thought I'd lost my mind! At the time, neither of us had a clue about why we were so intense about our perceptions (and demands!). But looking back twenty years later with the benefit of some hard-earned insight, we can see that our conflicts erupted because we had unknowingly dragged memories and perceptions about money from our past into our marriage. The mixture proved combustible!

As I've learned from many conversations with couples, Connie and I are the norm, not the exception. Let me identify a few contrasts I've noticed in couples:

- One is free spending; the other lives on a budget.

- One invests time and money in a business; the other wants to spend money on creating family memories.

- One is ambitious to advance in a career and is willing to move anywhere for the next promotion; the other longs for stability and rich, long-term relationships.

- One is generous; the other resents giving any money away.

- One is cautious and analytical; the other is impulsive.

- One feels exhilarated by taking risks; risks threaten the other.

- One wants to impart responsibility to the children; the other spoils them.

- One is dominating and demanding; the other is passive and compliant. (If you think that's the ideal situation, you're either the one who wants to dominate or you don't realize that passive people can still be furious under the surface.)

When Connie and I began to realize that many of our arguments were the product of intense convictions based on past hurts and hopes, we were able to be more objective about ourselves and each other, to give a little more grace and understanding, and to look for common ground instead of demanding our own way. Insight about the past has been a huge help for the present.

WISHING AND HOPING

Some of us have been looking for Santa Claus our whole lives. We may not believe in the "jolly old elf" any longer, but we still think we'll hit the lottery or find buried treasure in the back yard. But wishing and hoping won't cut it.

As we examine memories of money, we may uncover some of the most painful events in our lives. The hurt we feel certainly isn't comfortable or glamorous, so we shut it off and go back to the way things used to be.

Others, though, respond to the insights of looking back at memories of money and conclude, "So *that's* why I've acted that way for all these years! Now I can do something about it." That's how I hope all of us will respond. My goal for this chapter isn't morbid introspection and psychological analysis. Instead, my aim is to provide some handles on your current attitudes and actions with regard to money so that you can make any necessary changes.

> *"So that's why I've acted that way for all these years! Now I can do something about it."*

Some people will read this chapter and reply, "I need to call Mom and Dad to thank them for teaching me how to handle money." But some will respond, "I finally get it. I finally understand why I've felt and acted this way. And I finally grasp the issues that have caused such conflict in our marriage. But I'm just at the beginning. I need to understand even more."

Without insight, we seldom change. With insight, we have the opportunity to change. With a little courage, we can change course and take steps to move from passivity or impulsiveness to responsibility. The results will be more contentment and fulfillment than we ever dreamed possible.

FINDING TREASURE

All of us value—in fact, truly treasure—something or someone, and we devote time and attention to it. We may have very different treasures, and we may have very different means of fulfilling our dreams, but we are devoted to the thing that matters most to us. Some of us devote ourselves to success or comfort or popularity. Some are devoted to feed the hungry or cure a disease. And some are devoted to a person. The famous French philosopher and physicist, Blaise Pascal, observed this drive in all of us. He wrote, "All men seek happiness. This is without exception. Whatever different means they employ, they all tend to this end. The cause of some going to war, and of others avoiding it, is the same desire in both, attended with different views. This is the motive of every action of every man, even of those who hang themselves."

The question is: What treasure is worth the investment of our hearts, our lives, and our finances?

One of my favorite parables Jesus told is actually two parallel stories. Both of them talk about something of value. He said, "God's kingdom is like a treasure hidden in a field for years and then accidentally found by a trespasser. The finder is ecstatic—what a find!—and proceeds to sell everything he owns to raise money and buy that field. Or, God's kingdom is like a jewel merchant on the hunt for excellent pearls. Finding one that is flawless, he immediately sells everything and buys it" (Matthew 13:44-46).

In the first story, a man was walking along and found a treasure that had been hidden in a field. In that part of the world, armies marched and fought for centuries. When an army approached, people often buried their prized possessions in the ground to keep them safe. For some reason, this treasure had not been recovered. The man realized that the value of the treasure was so immense that he sold everything he had to buy the land.

The second story is about a merchant whose job and passion was finding prize pearls. One day, he found one so magnificent that he responded just like the wanderer: He sold all he had to buy the pearl.

In both stories, the value of the treasure prompted action that would be considered extreme if the treasure and pearl weren't so valuable. I believe the treasure and the pearl are Christ himself, who is so valuable that nothing compares to him. It's precisely at this point that many of us become confused. We realize that Christ's love, forgiveness, and acceptance are the most wonderful treasures in the world, but fear, anxiety, and selfishness focus our affections on us, not him. We live in tension, with emotions and values in conflict with each other. One of the purposes of this chapter is to clear away some of the confusion, to surface the long hidden perceptions that cloud our hearts, and to clarify the choice to treasure what matters most every day. As long as I'm in this life, I won't get it perfect, but with clearer insights, at least I'll see the choices to live for selfish goals or for Christ and his purposes.

How do we know what we really treasure? All we need to do is examine our thoughts and our dreams, and we'll clearly see our treasure. When I have a few minutes to think, where does my mind go? When I daydream about the future, what do I imagine? Too often, I think about looking good in someone's eyes—or more accurately, looking *better than that guy* in someone's eyes. But if my treasure is the approval of others, I'll always be a puppet dancing on a string, being pulled by a word of affirmation or a frown on someone's face. That's not being fully alive! No, there's another way to live. Jesus said that our time, thoughts, and resources could be devoted to what matters most in the universe! In fact, he invites us to be partners with him in the greatest adventure known to man: changing people's lives by helping them find the infinite treasure. He told his followers, "Don't hoard treasure down here where it gets eaten by moths and corroded by rust or—worse!—stolen by burglars. Stockpile treasure in heaven, where it's safe from moth and rust and burglars. It's obvious, isn't it? The place where your treasure is, is the place you will most want to be, and end up being" (Matthew 6:19-21).

Elisabeth Elliot often has piercing insight about the things of God. We are wise, she observes, to loosen our grip on money so our hands can grasp something far more valuable. In *Keep a Quiet Heart*, she wrote, "Money holds terrible power when it is loved. It can blind us, shackle us, fill us with anxiety and fear, torment our days and nights with misery, wear us out with chasing it. . . . Poverty has not been my experience, but God has allowed in the lives of each of us some sort of loss, the withdrawal of something we valued, in order that we may learn to offer ourselves a little more willingly, to allow the touch of death on one more thing we have clutched so tightly, and thus know fullness and freedom and joy that much sooner."[9]

As I learn to value the things God values, I live the richest, most rewarding, and most challenging life I can live. Sure, it'll be complicated, and there will be risks. That's what an adventure is all about! I've learned that life is not as simple as some folks suggest—it's more like a twisted mystery at times. In the struggle, Christ has promised that his Spirit will guide us, even when we aren't aware of his presence.

> *I've learned that life is not as simple as some folks suggest—it's more like a twisted mystery at times.*

Our memories of money can be an important benchmark to help us take stock of our lives, assess what we've valued, and begin to reorient ourselves so that our lives reflect more and more what we really treasure.

---

9   Elisabeth Elliott, *Keep a Quiet Heart*, (Revell, 2004), pp. 38-39.

Think about it...

1. What are some memories about money that come to mind...

   —when you were a small child?

   —when you earned an allowance or worked to earn money as a youngster?

   —when you earned your first real paycheck?

2. For each of these, what are some ways your experiences affect your attitudes and choices about money today?

3. On a scale of 0 (not at all) to 10 (incredibly well), how well did your parents model wisdom and responsibility about managing money? Explain your answer.

4. Whether you learned lessons about money from your parents *because of* them or *in spite of* them, what are some of those lessons? How did you learn each of them?

5. If you are married, do any of the contrasts listed in that section fit you and your spouse? If so, describe the tension and conflict this difference can cause.

6. Do the exercises about your memories (the first two questions in this "Think about it...") and the insights in this chapter help you "connect the dots" between your past experiences and your present attitudes and actions regarding finances? Explain your answer.

7. How might these insights give you a platform for genuine change?

Going Deeper

1. If a completely objective person watched you for a week, what would that person conclude that you truly treasure? Explain your answer.

2. Read Matthew 13:44-46. What does it mean for us to "sell everything" to buy the field and the pearl?

3. What would that look like in your life? Is that attractive to you? Why or why not?

3 | Powered by Purpose

"I don't want to die for nothing. I want to die for something."
—Jack Bauer, 24

A few months ago, I watched one of the most amazing interviews I've ever seen. A national conference scheduled U2's Bono to talk about his commitment to relieving the HIV/AIDS epidemic in Africa. To be honest, I thought he'd be the typical, self-absorbed rock star who mouthed a few platitudes but really didn't have his heart in it. I was wrong. Really wrong. With crystal clarity, Bono explained that his celebrity status is "insane," but he wants to use it to accomplish something noble. He said that the church hasn't been doing its part. He isn't upset with Christ, he explained, but with Christians who claim to know Jesus but who don't care about the things Jesus cared about. Bono quoted the passage in Matthew 25 about feeding the hungry, caring for the sick, and visiting prisoners. In these verses, Jesus said that when we care for "the least of these my brothers," we are actually doing it for him. The sign of a true Christian, Bono insisted, is the commitment to take action to relieve suffering. He has devoted his fortune, his time and energy, and his reputation to the monumental task of wiping out the AIDS epidemic in Africa, and he's already making a profound difference.

As I watched the interview, I was struck with the biting insight that God has given me tremendous resources, too (not as much as

Bono, but plenty), and I can choose to use everything I am and everything I own to make a difference in other people's lives. When that interview began, I certainly didn't expect the words of a rock star to penetrate my soul and inspire me to action. Bono's interview was the tipping point to encourage me to write this book to help others connect their resources to what matters most.

We don't have to have great wealth or a worldwide reputation to make a difference. All we need is heart. My wife Connie has been an elementary school teacher for 20 years, and her heart is in tune with Bono's and Jesus'. Every year, I watch her devote herself to those young students. She genuinely cares for them as little people with hopes and hurts, dreams and fears. After 20 years, she could put herself on autopilot, but she doesn't. She still prepares for each day like it's the most important day in those children's lives. Over and over, I've seen her cry because a child is having difficulties at home, and Connie empathizes with that child's pain. Parents tell me how much their children love Connie, and they talk about how their kids love to go to school and learn because Connie loves them and makes school an adventure for them. Do you remember your kindergarten teacher? These kids will remember theirs, and many of them will do a little better in school and in life because an obscure kindergarten teacher cared enough to pour her life and her love into them.

Some people may be reading this book and feel a bit frustrated by now. They're thinking, *We're in the third chapter, but we haven't gotten into budgeting and investing yet. When is this guy going to get where I want to go?* If you're feeling frustrated that we aren't moving faster, I want to assure you that we'll get to all the details of financial management you can handle. But I've found that most people's choices with finances only make sense when they're moving in a clear, purposeful direction. If you try to make those decisions without a sense of purpose for your life, you'll be easily sidetracked and end up confused and empty. Defining or clarifying your sense

Defining or clarifying your sense of purpose is an essential element—actually, the essential element—in financial planning.

of purpose is an essential element—actually, *the* essential element—in financial planning. The needle on the compass of your life directs everything you are, everything you do, and everything you have.

DEAD ENDS

A few years ago, Connie and I took a vacation to Washington, D.C., and northern Virginia. I love history, and we enjoy visiting grand houses, so two of our stops were to George Washington's Mt. Vernon and Thomas Jefferson's Monticello. After touring the homes and listening to the guides talk about these men, I realized they were very different personalities.

These two men fascinated me, so I studied their lives. I learned that Washington accepted the command of the Continental Army when that ragtag bunch had almost no hope against the British Redcoats, the most powerful army in the world. He risked everything for a cause that seemed doomed to fail, but his courage and resolution carried him and his men through long, difficult years of battle, death, disease, and bitter cold. As general and as the first president, Washington's nobility and integrity guided him and our country. Over and over, people wanted this great man to become more of a king than a president, but he always humbly gave power away instead of insisting on more. After two terms, he chose to step away from power when he could easily have been president for life. When Emperor Napoleon heard that Washington had voluntarily stepped down, he was amazed. Faced with the thought of doing the same thing, he remarked, "I am no Washington!"

Jefferson's crucial role in the founding of the country is undeniable. The beauty and power of his thoughts in the Declaration of Independence continue to inspire us today, but in his biography of John Adams, historian David McCullough describes a dark side in Jefferson's life. During Washington and Adams's administrations, Jefferson repeatedly schemed to tarnish Adams' reputation, though he denied any involvement in these activities at the time. Instead of nobility and integrity, Jefferson's political legacy reads more like Watergate.

In their financial dealings, Washington and Jefferson were poles apart. Both owned large plantations, and they experienced financial hardships in the early years of the country. Washington was disciplined and wise in his handling of money, and when he died, he had one of the wealthiest estates in the nation. In contrast, Jefferson spent money on frivolous things his entire life. His journals record lavish expenses for all manner of purchases, from the finest leather gloves to the best wines. To pay off his loans, Jefferson often sold slaves and broke up their homes. When he died, his estate was deeply in debt, and he left a legacy of selfishness, foolish spending, and shattered families.

William James wrote, "The greatest use of a life is to spend it for something that outlasts it." Sadly, many people follow the example of Jefferson more than Washington. When I meet with clients, I typically ask questions about what matters most to them. Sometimes, I hear descriptions of wonderful, compelling purposes that inspire me, but sometimes people tell me that all they want in life is to have more money to spend on themselves. These people may be relentlessly driven to achieve success at all costs, or they may have inherited their wealth and be able to indulge every whim. Either way, their self-absorption causes them to miss out on rich relationships, the joy and peace of real contentment, and the thrill of seeing their lives touch others. They may have a lot of money and a lot of passion to have even more, but their paths lead eventually to dead ends.

In my life (and I suspect I'm not alone in this), one of the biggest engines that propels me down the dead end roads is comparison. For years, I woke up every day consciously or subconsciously comparing the possessions and pleasures Connie and I had to what others had. My conclusion was that I needed a bigger house, a bigger car, a bigger bank account, and a bigger wife (just kidding, Connie). If others' successes and possessions are the measuring stick, nothing is ever good enough because we can always find people who have more and bigger stuff. Companies throw gas on this fire of misplaced desire when they give awards, accolades, and plaques that honor those who led the company in sales—even if they lost their families and their health in their drive to achieve. Company directors can tell who has "the comparison virus" and will sell their soul to be the top salesman so at the annual meeting, the boss will call them up on stage and say, "You are the best! Everybody, look at him (or her). This is what you can be if you work as hard." I know how all that works because I bought that line. I was consumed with comparison. I was winning awards and making a lot of money, but after a while, I felt completely emotionally bankrupt. I became clinically depressed—hopeless, helpless, and confused. Comparison rotted my soul.

It's important for all of us to spend our lives for something that outlasts it.

It's important for all of us to spend our lives for something that outlasts it. Whether we're currently buried in debt, barely above water, or bucks in the bank, but still worried, we can take steps to discover what's really meaningful to us.

LOVE AND LOYALTY

People and causes; love and loyalty. I believe those are the ingredients of a life of purpose. If we look past our selfish desires, we find people we love and causes that inspire our loyalty. That's what makes life worth living and keeps us from paths leading to a dead end. When I think of love and loyalty, soldiers come to mind. I've watched lots of documentaries of men at war, and whether fighting in World War II, Korea, Viet Nam, Iraq, or anywhere else, men in the trenches often say they joined to fight for our country and freedom (noble causes), but in the heat of battle, they fight, bleed, and die for the guy next to them in the foxholes.

The people we live for are usually under our roofs, but we may expand the circle of purpose to include individuals and groups that share our commitment to a noble cause. We may, like Bono, devote ourselves to relieve suffering or stop the spread of disease, or we may invest our time, energy, and money in building houses for the poor, caring for prisoners or the elderly, sharing the Good News about Christ, helping someone who's hungry or hurting, or any of hundreds of other noble efforts.

I've heard people say that we should be able to write our life's purpose on the back of a business card, but I think life's a bit more complicated than that. Most of us have many different responsibilities, so our purpose in life will reflect those complexities. If we're going to live for something or someone beyond ourselves, we can look at three areas of life:

First, we begin with our families.

A major part of my purpose is to provide for Connie and our kids—not just financially, but in every way that a good husband and father provides. Some of us may be tempted to dream big dreams for our lives—and I'm all for that—but the biggest dreams shouldn't bypass our most cherished relationships. At the end of my life, my dreams won't be nearly as important as the quality of relationships I've had with Connie, JR, Brandon, and Carissa. I may want a new Lexus and other expensive toys, and I can afford them—but not if I want to provide money for a college education for my kids, a nice wedding for Carissa, and some great vacations that make memories for a lifetime. Putting my family first means saying "no" to some things I'd really enjoy for a while, but that's okay with me because my family is an enduring treasure.

I'd like to say that I've always had this perspective, but that would be a lie. For years, I put my career first, spending my resources of time, money, and affections on building the biggest business I could build. I was driven to be a success, but in the back of my mind, I felt guilty and ashamed that I wasn't the husband and father I knew I could be. I came to a point that I finally saw the emptiness of my pursuits and the damage I was inflicting on those I loved. During that painful season, I faced reality and made the choice to value my family more than my own career. My only regret in that decision is that it took a while for me to "get it."

Next, we can examine our own lives and notice the activities that bring us the most fulfillment.

Those things that bring us the most joy and stimulate our passions are almost certainly part of our purpose in life. For example, a friend of mine is in a management position in his company, but he told me, "You know, I can manage schedules and work loads just fine, but what I really enjoy—what really revs my engines—is when I can build confidence and skills into people's lives. I love to see other people succeed!" He just described an important element in his life's purpose.

Some of us dream of making a difference beyond our normal sphere of influence.

Many of us are completely satisfied with providing for our families and using our abilities in fulfilling ways at work or in our communities, but we are wise to at least consider one more step: We can dream about touching countless lives if we step out of the normal way of doing life and go for even more. Certainly, most of us are not entrepreneurs. Many of us are quite content making a difference in our own spheres of life, but some of us long for a bigger impact. Something inside propels us to dream, like Bono, of gathering people and resources and making a huge difference in a community, a nation, or the world. Let me give you a few examples.

> *Something inside propels us to dream, like Bono, of gathering people and resources and making a huge difference in a community.*

- William Wilberforce was a homely little man who served in Britain's House of Parliament. After he became a Christian, he reflected on God's intention for his life. Soon, he was convinced of his purpose. He wrote perhaps the shortest and most challenging purpose statement I've ever read: "God Almighty has set before me two great objects, the suppression of the Slave Trade and the Reformation of Manners [turning people from vice to virtue]." England was the world's greatest sea power, and much of its commerce was built on the backs of slave labor. For this reason, powerful forces in government and industry opposed Wilberforce's efforts to free the slaves. He was sometimes physically beaten and often verbally ridiculed, but he was resolute in his purpose. Just days before he died, news reached him that a bill had passed to outlaw the slave trade. His purpose was fulfilled.

- On a more personal level, Phyllis Stanley wrote:

"I want to live my life very *purposely*, regularly reviewing and praying over my purpose in life, loving God intensely, cherishing and inspiring my husband, praying for and keeping connected spiritually with my children, loving women and seeking to lay spiritual foundations in their lives.

"I want to live *faithfully*, believing God for what I cannot see. I want to believe that God can do in my children's lives what I cannot do.

"I want to live *creatively*, creating beauty and warmth in my home, around my table, and in my Bible study. Creativity adds sparkle to a focused, purposeful life.

"I want to live *paradoxically*. I want to go against my selfish nature, against our culture, giving a little bit more than I feel like giving, going the second mile, being like Jesus."[10]

- And a friend of mine shared his purpose with me. It reads:

"After thinking about how I've experienced fulfillment and what I want people to say at my funeral, my purpose is:
  — That my family would be convinced that I genuinely love them.
  — That I provide adequately for them.
  — That I impart some measure of wisdom to my family, friends, and clients.
  — That I help people wrestle with the complexity of God and his will for us.
  — That I serve to deepen and extend people's God-given messages."

Our purpose statement doesn't have to follow anyone's direction or design. Far more importantly, it needs to come from our

---

10 Quoted by Linda Dillow in *Calm My Anxious Heart*, (Navpress, Colorado Springs, 1998), p. 105.

hearts. The ultimate direction for our lives seldom is clear at the beginning. Most of us need time and experience to refine our desires and discover the things that matter most to us. Stephen Covey, author of the best-seller, *Seven Habits of Highly Effective People,* wrote, "Whatever is at the center of our life will be the source of our security, guidance, wisdom, and power."

AUTHENTICITY AND ACTION

Things have changed since the 18th century when Wilberforce trusted God to use him to free the slaves. Today, the obstacles to fulfilling our purposes aren't governments and industries. We face the soul numbing multiple effects of incredible disposable wealth, the rapid speed of life, a vast array of options for any decision, and relativism that tells us that all choices are equally valid. The sheer quantity of choices we face each day is mind-boggling. For example, only a few years ago, television offered only three networks, but today, cable or dish TV offers hundreds of options for every hour of the day. Technology has made even the most obscure information available in a heartbeat, and we can communicate with each other with startling ease.

In addition to the vast amounts of money, technology, and comforts we enjoy, spectacular failures in government, business, and the church have eroded trust in authority. We may conclude that wealth, the speed of life, relativism, and being cynical of authority have shattered people's sense of purpose, but they haven't. They're just looking for something they can really believe in. Today, people long for and look for authenticity. They don't care what anyone promises (they hear promises all day, every day). They want to know if people are authentic, with integrity and gut-level honesty, and willing to admit when they don't have all the answers.

People who value authenticity don't want to just write a purpose statement in a notebook. They want to take action. If they say their purpose is to help homeless people, they go downtown to take some food and clothes to people who live under bridges. If they commit themselves to teach children of immigrants to read, they carve out substantial time to do the research, find the best methods and organizations, and go to these children to teach them new skills.

Many young people I meet realize the "opportunity costs" of their choice where they invest their lives, so they take a little extra time to consider the implications of their decisions. They understand that when they say "yes" to one mission, they're saying "no" to countless others. They have a finite amount of time and money, so they want to be sure that they are investing in the things that really matter. Years ago, people trusted authority more than they do today, and they were willing to be told which direction to go. But no longer. This generation researches the options, weighs the possible outcomes, and makes decisions based on gut-level instinct and input from peers.

Purpose isn't stagnant. Few of us have a single, compelling purpose throughout our lives like Wilberforce. For most of us, our sense of direction and passion shifts as we uncover new abilities and discover new responsibilities and opportunities. As the years go by, our purpose may seem more clouded at one time than another, but hopefully, it will become clearer as we actively engage in things that stimulate our interests and awaken our souls.

> *For most of us, our sense of direction and passion shifts as we uncover new abilities and discover new responsibilities and opportunities.*

Older generations sometimes could articulate a clear purpose, but too often, they failed to put their resources into action to make a real difference, or their personal lives failed to match up with their stated purposes. Today's generation is looking for something authentic, something rich and real, and something more than pious statements that they can pour their lives into. They want their lives to count in tangible ways.

As we've been saying in these first three chapters, uncovering and clarifying what matters most gives direction to every area of our lives, including financial planning. A clear, compelling purpose captures our hearts. We get up every day (or most days, anyway) with a sense that our lives are going to count for something beyond our own selfish demands. That's fantastic! Our purpose energizes us and makes us want to use every resource we possess to make a difference in the lives of our family, our work, our neighborhood, and in any cause that makes our hearts sing.

No matter what our financial condition might be, establishing a clear purpose is an important step in providing motivation for change. Those who are buried in debt will realize that they've been hustling down the wrong path, and now they can change direction. First, they can take steps to get out of debt so they will be free to pursue their purpose with enthusiasm and passion. Those who are barely above water will grasp the fact that real life is a lot more than just getting by. With a strong, new sense of direction, they'll be motivated to make better choices to provide for the future and accomplish their life's mission. Those who have bucks in the bank but are still worried will have their worries melt away in the warmth of confidence in God and in their future. And those who are full of purpose and contentment will continue to help others find and follow real meaning in life with even more clarity.

TRANSCENDENCE

One of the refreshing elements of the younger generation's view of life is that they ask tough questions without assuming the answers. This unnerves some of us, but it encourages us to look at things from a fresh perspective. They're willing to ask questions like, "If God exists, what difference does he make in my life? Does he have any claim on me? Does he really have a purpose for me?"

Actually, those are questions seekers have asked for millennia. Answers can be elusive, but author Os Guinness has concluded that if God indeed exists, and if he is involved in our lives, then surely his purposes permeate every fiber of our existence. In his insightful and challenging book, *The Call*, Guinness defines our purpose as "the truth that God calls us to himself so decisively that everything we are, everything we do, and everything we have is invested with a special devotion and dynamism lived out as a response to his summons and service."[11]

---

11   Os Guinness, *The Call*, (Word Publishing, Nashville, 1998), p. 4.

We live in a tangible world, and to a large degree, our existence is dominated by what we can see, feel, hear, taste, and smell. But God "has put eternity in our hearts," and we instinctively know there's something beyond the tangible. The unseen world is every bit as real as the seen, and we long for the invisible to make a difference in our lives. The perspectives and convictions we absorb as we "reach for the invisible God" give us direction for our choices in the visible world of relationships, work, time, and money.

Certainly, throughout history, some people have lived meaningful lives apart from God. They have cared for the poor, built libraries, provided medical care, educated children, and performed a host of other noble works. But apart from the centerpiece of a transcendent purpose, one that is defined and guided by God himself, people often slip back into a self-absorbed existence. Instead of the thrill and challenge of changing lives, they experience nagging emptiness punctuated by fleeting moments of elation.

But we can't just add Jesus to our already full lives. Christ didn't come to help us be more successful in our selfish pursuits. He came to revolutionize our lives, to give us love for the unlovely and broken hearts for the hardhearted. If he is truly who he says he is—the Savior who forgives and the Almighty God who spoke and created the universe with a word—then he commands our wonder and devotion. If we're looking for love and loyalty to drive us, for a person and a cause that inspire us, then we need look no further than Jesus.

> *If we're looking for love and loyalty to drive us, for a person and a cause that inspire us, then we need look no further than Jesus.*

Jesus didn't try to make following him sound easy. His purpose brings far more fulfillment than anything else life can offer, but his path leads us through valleys as well as to mountaintops, full of challenges as well as thrills. He told his followers, "Anyone who intends to come with me has to let me lead. You're not in the driver's seat; I am. Don't run from suffering; embrace it. Follow me and I'll show you how. Self-help is no help at all. Self-sacrifice is the way, my way, to finding yourself, your true self. What kind of deal is it to get everything you want but lose yourself? What could you ever trade your soul for?" (Matthew 16:24-26)

Jesus was communicating "the paradox of purpose": If we pursue self-fulfillment, we'll end up empty, but if we give our lives away, we'll experience love, peace, joy, and tremendous satisfaction. Self-absorption, Jesus assured us, guarantees an empty life. We may get everything we want, but we lose what's most important and most fulfilling: rich relationships and the thrill of seeing that our lives really count. But purpose is personal. As we read the Scriptures and pursue God's direction for our lives, he will give each of us light and life, but his purpose will be uniquely crafted according to our personalities, our abilities and passions, and the opportunities he gives us right where we live.

Often people ask, "Just how does it work? How does God show us our purpose?" Those are great questions, and the answers aren't that simple. We may want something dramatic, but God usually shows us his path for us in more humble ways. For every Moses who saw a burning bush, there are a million others whose purpose is clarified bit by bit and day by day as we read the Scriptures to learn more about God's character and his plan, as we pray for God's leading, as we increasingly tune our hearts to sense the Holy Spirit's prompting and nudging, and as we trust God to open doors of opportunity. When we take steps of faith, we realize that we're good at some things, but not so good at others. Our friends and leaders affirm what they see in us, and we feel encouraged by their input. No, this process isn't nearly as exciting as seeing a burning bush or hearing an audible voice, but that's the way God leads the vast majority of us as we pursue a purpose that lines up with God's. As that purpose captures our hearts, we'll use every resource in our lives to fulfill it.

One of the biggest benefits of clarifying our purpose is that we can learn to rest. Rich, real wisdom doesn't come our way when we're flying through life at 90 miles an hour. For many people I meet with, life feels like a runaway freight train. When Moses came down from the mountain with the Ten Commandments, one of them told us to stop regularly to reflect, think, and talk about what matters most. That's a lesson we still need to learn today. No amount of religious activity can replace the benefits of rest. One of the most important insights men and women can learn in our culture is the absolute necessity of changing pace, slowing down, and reflecting about the most meaningful things in our lives.

For years, I measured the meaning of my life by the number of things on my to-do list and the names in my appointment book. The more the better. And in fact, I was only satisfied if I had to rush from place to place with no time in between. In his article, "Diagnosing Hurry Sickness," in *Leadership* magazine, popular author John Ortberg identified two signs of stress—speeding up and multi-tasking:

- "Speeding up. You are haunted by the fear that you don't have enough time to do what needs to be done. You try to read faster, lead board meetings more efficiently, write sermons on the fly, and when counseling, you nod more often to encourage the counselee to accelerate."

- "Multiple-tasking. You find yourself doing or thinking more than one thing at a time. The car is a favorite place for this. Hurry-sick pastors [and anyone else, for that matter] may drive, eat, drink coffee, listen to tapes for sermon ideas, shave or apply make-up, direct church business on the car phone—all at the same time. Or they may try to watch TV, read *Leadership,* eat dinner, and carry on a phone conversation simultaneously."[12]

Hurry sickness is an epidemic in our culture. It promises success, but robs us of meaning. One of the most courageous things any of us can do is face our compulsion to hurry and take bold steps to stop, rest, and reflect. Try it. It'll change your life.

---

12 John Ortberg, "Diagnosing Hurry Sickness," *Leadership,* Fall, 1998.

Big Dreams, Big Hearts

Early in my career, I was driven to become a success. At that time, I thought ambition was the highest virtue in anyone's life. Later, when I began following Jesus, I became much more suspicious of ambition—especially my own. Ambition, though, is neutral. The drive to achieve can be right or wrong, good or bad, depending on the purpose. If it's noble, then ambition can be shaped and directed by love and loyalty instead of self-promotion.

I've learned that it's wise to be cautious about great goals and big dreams. After all, Jesus said, "The meek [not power-hungry people] shall inherit the earth." Those who have bigger dreams must wrestle with pride and humility, and humility comes from being broken, the painful process of realizing that our selfish ambitions are stubborn and insatiable. When stubbornness gives way to authentic love and compassion, God's grace (coupled with our genuine efforts) produces love, joy, and peace in our lives. This delicious fruit can never be earned or achieved by our power alone.

> *Humility comes from being broken, the painful process of realizing that our selfish ambitions are stubborn and insatiable.*

Strong leadership and a bold vision can't be thrust on people by a megalomaniac. Loyalty must be earned. In his book, *In, But Not Of: A Guide to Christian Ambition and the Desire to Influence the World*, author Hugh Hewitt wants to see Christians "consciously commit to impacting the culture. To do that requires influence. Influence is not an automatic gift bestowed on good people. It is earned."[13]

I believe God delights when we dream big dreams that focus on his purposes and trust his means to accomplish those goals, but spiritual words don't guarantee noble hearts. We all know about Christian charlatans who use dramatic, emotional language about

---

13 Reviewed by Gina R. Dalfonzo, www.boundless.org/2002_2003/departments/pages/a0000800.html

God to manipulate people to give money to build bigger buildings and pay for huge salaries. Today, I'm more suspicious of people who have grand, glowing dreams, and I look for authenticity in their words and actions. My pastor, Rick Baldwin, is one of the best examples of someone with big dreams and a big heart. He often talks about the reason he and a group of people started our church nine years ago. He did the research, and he realized that 250,000 people who don't go to any church live within 30 minutes of our building. And when he talks about reaching them with the love and forgiveness of Christ, he almost always has tears in his eyes. I've been around him enough to know that his tears are genuine. He really cares for people. He's a man of big dreams who is energized and directed by love, not selfish ambition. He's a man with a big heart. Rick is a man who is powered by purpose.

TENACITY

Many factors threaten our sense of purpose. Selfishness can erode it, and disappointments can make us want to give up. Those who experience fulfillment are usually those who have faced difficulty and loss, but they eventually achieved their purpose. Some writers even say that "the death of a dream" is an integral part of the process of reconstructing, redefining, and resurrecting that dream.

Guideposts can help us stay on the path when we are tempted to drift or run away. Jonathan Edwards was a Christian leader with a powerful sense of destiny. To keep on track, he wrote a series of resolutions to guide his life. Some of these include:

"Resolved, to live with all my might, while I do live.
Resolved, never to lose one moment of time; but improve it
    the most profitable way I possibly can.
Resolved, never to do any thing out of revenge.
Resolved, never to do anything, which I should be afraid to
    do, if it were the last hour of my life."

One of the strongest statements of tenacity is found in a poem by Robert Service, who wrote about the hardships and grit of miners who searched for gold in the Yukon. Through bitter cold and harsh deprivations, these men and a few women kept their focus. In "The Law of the Yukon," Service wrote:

> "Send not your foolish and feeble; send me your strong and your sane,
> Strong for the red-rage of battle, sane for I harry them sore.
> Send me men girt for the combat, men who are grit to the core. . . .
> And I wait for the men who will win me—and I will not be won in a day,
> And I will not be won by weaklings, subtle and suave and mild,
> But by men with the hearts of Vikings and the simple faith of a child,
> Desperate, strong, and resistless, unthrottled by fear or defeat,
> Them will I gild with my treasure, them will I glut with my meat."[14]

Few of us face the hardships these miners endured, but all of us can learn from them to be more dedicated to our goal and tenacious in achieving it.

First Steps

Most of us aren't quite ready to leave home and devote the rest of our lives to a cause in another land. Our first steps are much closer to home, and in fact, are probably at our homes. We don't need to be dreaming big dreams until we are taking responsibility to care for those who are in front of us every day.

In *Keep a Quiet Heart*, author Elisabeth Elliott tells the story of a friend who took his first steps to fulfill his purpose. Elliott wrote, "My friend Jim O'Donnell tells how he, a hard-headed, hard-hearted man of the world, found Christ. His conscience was awakened.

---

[14] "The Law of the Yukon," by Robert W. Service, quoted by Elisabeth Elliott in *The Path of Loneliness* (Servant Publications, Grand Rapids, Michigan, 2001), pp. 105-106.

The call of God was immediate: 'Go home and love your wife.' The change was so sudden and so radical, Lizzie could not make head or tail of what had come over him. This self-confident and self-interested man had quit living for himself. He had died. An altogether new kind of life was now his. The first difference it made was the difference that mattered most—in his private life."[15]

We've spent three chapters looking at our memories, our values, and our purpose in life. Does all this make any difference in how we handle our money? Yes, it makes all the difference in the world! Even when our sense of purpose is still in the process of being clarified, it gives us enthusiasm and energy to connect every resource in our lives to what matters most. That's the way we make our money count.

In the next chapter, you'll get to chart out your plan. The thought of writing your financial plan gives some of you goose bumps, but some of you are going catatonic at the thought—and the two of you are probably married to each other! I want to encourage you to pour your heart into the next chapter or two. Don't see it as a meaningless exercise. It's not! In fact, the plan you chart in the next couple of chapters can bring you more peace and fulfillment than you ever dreamed possible. After that, we'll look at some amazing facts about saving and investing in Chapter 6. Hang on. It's going to be a fun ride!

In fact, the plan you chart in the next couple of chapters can bring you more peace and fulfillment than you ever dreamed possible.

---

15 Elisabeth Elliott, *Keep a Quiet Heart*, (Revell, 2004), p. 156.

THINK ABOUT IT...

This exercise is designed to help you clarify what matters most to you so that you can write a purpose statement for your life...and your money.

1. Make a list of your strengths (in relationships, at work, in every aspect of your life).

2. Block out your life into 10-year increments. Actually, start with a 5-year period of your late adolescence (15-20 years old), and then cover each decade of your adulthood. In each period, list the activities that brought you the most joy and fulfillment. Then, for each of those activities, identify the particular aspect of it that gave you a sense of fulfillment.

3. After answering the questions about the activities that brought fulfillment and frustration, look for a pattern of fulfillment. What would you say is your life's "hot spot," the activities that have been the most fulfilling?

4. Who or what has helped shape the direction of your life toward the things that bring the most fulfillment?

5. If someone asked your best friends or family about you, what would they say is your purpose in life? Explain your answer.

6. Imagine listening to people as they talk about you at your funeral. What do you hope they will say about you? And think about God's summary of your life at that moment. What would cause Him to say, "Well done, good and faithful servant. Enter into the joy of your Master"?

7. Did any of the purpose statements in the chapter seem to fit you? If so, describe what elements of it were most encouraging to you.

8. Reflect on the things that have given you a sense of fulfillment and the legacy you want to leave behind. As clearly as possible, write a statement of your life's purpose. (It doesn't matter how long it is, and if it isn't as clear today as you want it to be, that's okay. Most of us spend a lifetime clarifying and shaping our sense of purpose. Think deeply, reflect on the things that mean most to you, and write your purpose statement.)

9. How does your purpose in life affect how you use your resources? In other words, how can you connect your resources to what matters most to you? What difference will this make in how you handle your finances and other resources?

GOING DEEPER
1. Read Matthew 16:24-26. What do you think it means to "lose your life" so you can "find it"?

2. Plenty of people want to "get everything they want." What are some evidences that they actually "lose" out on life by pursuing that goal?

3. In what extent would you say your purpose in life is connected to God's purposes? Explain your answer. What are some specific ways you can align your purpose more with God's?

4. What would your life look like if you were convinced "that everything you are, everything you do, and everything you have is invested with a special devotion and dynamism lived out as a response to God's summons and service"?

4 | The Blueprint for Financial Success

"Unless commitment is made, there are only promises and hopes . . . but no plans." —Peter Drucker

Rafe and Liz had been dreaming about building a new house since they got married fifteen years ago. When they went on vacations, they often drove through nice neighborhoods in distant cities to get more ideas. They devoured magazines for design concepts for houses and landscaping, and they talked endlessly about the kind of house they wanted to build. Thinking about their dream house was almost a game to them, and they enjoyed it.

During those years, Rafe was promoted several times, and each time, they got a little closer to the point of saying "yes" to build their home. Then, Liz received an inheritance from her grandmother's estate, just enough to give them a sizable down payment. That did it. They were ready!

They kicked their planning into high gear. Instead of dreams, they now started making plans. Suddenly, they realized they had to make some decisions—some hard decisions—about what's most important to them. They quickly understood that those years of dreaming about their ideal home would have to be tempered by the reality that they couldn't do everything they'd ever wanted to do.

After all, people worth millions of dollars owned many of the houses they'd seen. Rafe and Liz had significant resources, but not millions.

Liz loved to entertain, so having a nice dining room was important to her. Their daughter was in middle school, and their son was in the fourth grade. Rafe enjoyed playing soccer and baseball with his son, so he wanted a big backyard. They both wanted their bedroom to be a long way from the kids' rooms. They looked at plans for a 4000 square foot house that had a large dining room, but if they built their house that large, they could only afford a small lot that wasn't in the school district where they wanted to live. As the days went by, they had to talk through their hopes and dreams, and they both had to be willing to compromise. After weeks of long and occasionally intense conversations, they realized that one of their biggest priorities was a game room. Their children would be in middle school and high school in the coming years, and they wanted a place where they could bring their friends to hang out. The process of planning may have dampened some of their dreams, but it crystallized their real desires for their family.

They hired a builder who had some great house plans, and they were able to tell him exactly what they could afford and what they wanted. Soon, they decided on a plan, and they picked a neighborhood that wasn't what they had dreamed about, but it fit their newly clarified goals.

The process Rafe and Liz experienced in building a home is a perfect analogy to creating a sound, effective financial plan. For that reason, I call this process "The Blueprint for Financial Success."

> *Blundering along in life without a plan is a sure way to raise levels of anxiety, fear, confusion, and tension between family members.*

WHAT DIFFERENCE DOES IT MAKE?

When we talk about financial plans, some people roll their eyes and think, *Good grief. That sounds so boring!* But having a workable plan is essential to a life of peace, contentment, and fulfillment. Blundering along in life without a plan is a sure way to raise levels of anxiety, fear, confusion, and tension between family members. It takes a little work, but the benefits are enormous! Before we get into the process, let me tell you about a few people who found it helpful.

- Suzanne is a single mom who was buried in debt. She was raising two children on a job that didn't pay well. She came to my office and shared her hopes and dreams. As we talked, I asked her about her goals as well as her assets, liabilities, and expenses. One of the things she really wanted to do was to take her sons on a nice vacation to Europe. That was her dream, but she didn't see any way that could happen. Her first goal was to get out of debt.

One of Suzanne's expenses was smoking cigarettes. We calculated that she was spending $40 a week on cigarettes. "I've tried to quit," she told me, "but I guess I haven't been too motivated." I showed her that by saving the $40 a week, she'd have over $2000 in a year. For some reason, this reality had never dawned on her. Actually, we found several other expenses that she could eliminate, like cable television and some magazine subscriptions, and in the end, she chose to keep cable but drop the magazines.

As the year went by, Suzanne was able to pay off $1500 in debts, and a year after she came to see me, she took her boys on a vacation to the beach in Florida. When she got back, she called to tell me, "Jim, it wasn't Europe, but we had a great time together. And I feel even better because I'm not in debt any more. Thank you!"

- Robert and Rebekah had a bunch of fun friends, and they tried to do everything their friends could afford. They took nice cruises with them, Robert bought the finest fishing gear so he would look good when he went with his buddies, and Rebekah shopped at upscale stores with her friends. When they came to see me, they were a classic case of living barely above water. They had gone years without owing any money, but they spent every dime they earned. Recently, some medical bills had put them over the edge, and they realized that something needed to change.

As we talked, they realized they were locked into the lifestyle they were living. They needed an emergency fund and some investments for the future, but these choices conflicted with their deep desire to maintain their spending levels so they could keep up with their friends. We outlined what matters most to them, and they finally decided that the peace of having a cushion outweighed (but just barely) their desire to keep spending to be accepted by their friends. We designed a budget, and with only a few changes (from my perspective) about some important expenses (from their perspective), they were able to put hundreds of dollars each month into an emergency savings fund and then into a mutual fund. A year later, they came to see me, and they were thrilled! They felt great about their growing nest egg, and Rebekah explained, "When I told my friends what Robert and I were doing to save money, several of them decided to do the same things. They were as afraid of losing friends as we'd been, so we made changes together."

- Six years ago, Steven was in his mid-30s, and he had a dream. He always had a knack for technology, and he had been tinkering with a new device that would make offset printing cheaper but with higher quality. He patented his invention, and he took his concept to investment bankers in New York. They loved the idea, and they backed him in creating a new company.

Steven was, to say the least, dedicated to his new company. He flew all over the country meeting with printing companies, and he often flew to New York to meet with his investors. When he was in town, he regularly worked 16- or 18-hour days, 6 or 7 days a week. His company was doing well . . . very well.

When Steven came to see me, his company was five years old. That year, it had grossed over $100 million, and his personal net worth had skyrocketed to $50 million. But the day before, his wife had contacted an attorney to start divorce proceedings, and his children despised him so much they refused to talk to him. Steven was distraught, but he was so immersed in running his business, his cell phone never stopped ringing during the hour we talked. From the look on his face, I realized he needed more than a little financial advice. He needed a complete change in his life's priorities.

I met with Steven several times to talk about what matters most to him. He realized that his preoccupation with his career and money was costing him the people he loved most. The reality of their hostility shattered him, and one day, he called to tell me he was thinking of taking his life. A few minutes later, we met, and I took him to see a counselor. In the weeks that followed, some amazing things happened. Steven mustered the courage to make changes—not superficial ones, but drastic ones. He hired someone to take over his business as the CEO, and he became the board chairman with far fewer responsibilities. He asked his wife and children for forgiveness, and he made it his aim to earn their trust and respect again. That road had many ups and downs, but eventually, his marriage was restored. One of his children now cherishes her father, but the other hasn't yet found the faith to trust him.

No amount of money and no level of business success could fill the hole in Steven's soul. He had almost lost everything, but a hard look at his life enabled him to make decisions to reclaim what mattered most to him.

- From time to time, people come to my office who inspire me. When I ask them the questions about their life's purpose, their eyes light up, and they tell me about the passion that gets them up each morning and keeps them from sleeping at night because they are so excited about it. Charles and Diane are like that. When I met with them, they told me about their work with the homeless. They don't just donate money. They give generously of their funds, but they give even more of their time and their hearts. Diane told me, "Jim, you have no idea how it thrills me to be able to help a young mother on the street who desperately needs food and medical care for her baby."

Diane and Charles explained that they got into this work almost by accident, but it captured their hearts. A group from their church asked Charles to drive the youth group's van so they could take some food and clothes to homeless people. Diane went along for the ride. Neither of them realized how God would touch their hearts that day. They are well connected, so they garnered resources and commitments from a number of churches and social organizations. In addition to food and clothes, they are providing job training and placement, reading skills, and courses in self-protection. Today, they are making a huge difference in hundreds of lives.

Why, you might ask, did they come to see me? Charles told me, "We want to maximize our impact with those dear people, and we want you to help us." Gladly, sir, gladly.

Financial planning may begin with a commitment to responsibility, but it results in tremendous satisfaction. A friend told me about the sheer delight of providing for his now grown children. He said, "When my kids were little, I wanted to be sure they had a good education. I knew I couldn't afford to send them to an expensive college, but I wanted to at least send them to a state university. My wife and I started a college fund for them, and by the time they went to college, we had enough. I remember the enormous sense of satisfaction when I wrote that first check for my daughter's tuition, room, and board. And I felt the same way every semester for her four years and my son's four years, too. I had done what I set out to do, and it felt great!"

Financial planning may begin with a commitment to responsibility, but it results in tremendous satisfaction.

An Overview

The Blueprint has three sections: defining what matters most to you, a snapshot of your current financial position, and setting specific goals for your future. In the first three chapters of this book, we focused on your vision and identified what matters most. That's crucial, but it's only the first step. In this chapter, we'll be *intentional* by setting goals, and in the remaining chapters, we'll examine the nuts and bolts, the *means* of achieving your goals.

Setting goals is an important step that will guide our decisions about money. For most of us, our goals include our children's college education, weddings, family vacations, retirement, a cause that inspires us, and perhaps a significant hobby. Some people may want to save enough to start their own business or buy a boat or a vacation home. And some people need to have enough money to adopt a child or provide extensive medical care for a family member.

The Blueprint isn't magical, and it isn't strange. It's a straightforward look at those three elements of an effective financial plan, and it prepares you to take steps to accomplish your specific goals and fulfill your dreams.

Okay, we're ready. Get your pencil out, and let's get started.

THE BLUEPRINT FOR FINANCIAL SUCCESS

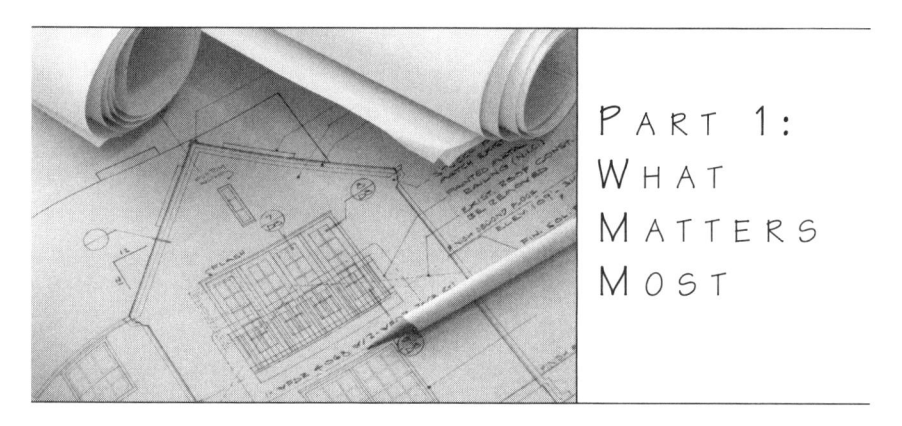

PART 1: WHAT MATTERS MOST

Based on the reflection you've done in the first three chapters…

- What and who matter most to you?

- How do finances relate to what matters most to you?

- What is your experience, good and bad, with money and investments? (Reflecting on your financial experiences is a good first step as you design a workable plan to connect your resources to what matters most.)

Common purposes...or not.
Opposites attract, and quite often, a husband and wife have very different ways of responding to risk and making decisions. These differences are actually a strength of the relationship because each person complements and balances the other.
- Would your friends say you make decisions quickly, or would they say you are very cautious and analytical? What would they say about how your spouse makes decisions?

- In what ways do your answers about what matters most *complement* or *compete with* your spouse's answers?

- Regarding financial issues, who is the decision-maker in the family? Would your spouse agree?

- Describe any common sources of tension in how you and your spouse handle money.

PART 2:
CURRENT
FINANCIAL
POSITION

In this section of the Blueprint, you take a snapshot of your current financial position. Be rigorously honest and make an accurate assessment. When I work with clients, I ask them to bring every piece of information that has to do with their money: bank statements, IRAs, 401k's, other investments, mortgage information, auto loans, credit card balances and other debts, and all sources of income and a copy of the budget if they have one.

One client asked me if he should include some family debts. That's a good question, and one that's not easily answered. Many people fail to list money they've borrowed from family members as debts they owe. Somehow, they seem to think it doesn't really count—and it doesn't if they don't intend to repay it, except in their consciences. Similarly, many people don't list money owed to them by family members as assets because, I assume, they aren't sure they'll be paid back. The point here is that there's no need to list money owed by you or to you if there's little chance of it being paid. I would, however, encourage people to make a commitment to pay back any money borrowed from parents, siblings, friends, or employers. They may have given up on it, but they'll be glad to be surprised by your check!

Let me give you an example of a snapshot of a couple's financial position. John and Krista are in their early 30s with two small children. Both of them worked until their first child was born. Krista put her career on hold to be at home, but their income, of course, was cut in half. When they came to see me, they realized they needed to plan effectively so they could provide for their family. First, they articulated what matters most. They told me that they have two passions: their family and their volunteer work at a food pantry.

The next step for John and Krista was to take a snapshot of their finances. Here's what they listed under "assets":

- Checking account: $2525

- Emergency savings account: $3400

- John's 401k: $58,560

- Krista's 401k: $22,985

- Intel stock given to Krista by her father: $15,300

- Mutual funds: $17,775

- Market value of their home: $205,000

- Cash value of Krista's life insurance policy: $16,150

- Blue book value of John's car: $4500

- Blue book value of Krista's van: $14,700

    The total of their assets was $360,895.

Soon after they were married, John was able to pay off his college loans and pay for his car. Under liabilities, they listed:
- Auto loan on Krista's van: $13,290
- Credit card debt: $500
- Mortgage on their home: $165,455

    The total of their liabilities was $179,245.

    Their net worth came to $181,650.

Now it's your turn. List every asset and liability:

Assets
- Cash (savings, checking account, money market accounts, CDs, etc.)

    _____

    _____

    _____

- Investments (401K or 403B, IRA, Roth IRA, brokerage accounts, UGMA, etc.)

    _____

    _____

    _____

    _____

- Other assets (real estate, business equity, vehicles, personal property, etc.)

    _____

    _____

MAKE YOUR MONEY COUNT

- Total Assets:

  _____

Liabilities
- Debts (home mortgage, auto loans, credit card debt, other debt)

  _____

  _____

  _____

  _____

- Total Liabilities

  _____

- Assets minus Liabilities equals Net worth

  _____

  For budgeting purposes, list salaries as the annual income for your family.
- Monthly or Annual Income

  Name:_____Income:_____

  Name:_____Income:_____

- Monthly or Annual Expenses

  Name: _____ Expenses: _____

  Name: _____ Expenses: _____

- Monthly surplus or deficit: _____
- Annual surplus or deficit: _____

Part 3: Specific Financial Goals

Some of us are gifted at setting good, clear goals, but others need some help. Popular author and speaker Brian Tracy wrote, "Successful men and women invest the time necessary to develop absolute clarity about themselves and what they really want, like designing a detailed blueprint for a building before they begin construction. Most people just throw themselves at life like a dog chasing a passing car and wonder why they never seem to catch anything or keep anything worthwhile."[16]

As you consider your goals, think about these principles:

- Goals must be your own. Don't just adopt your parents' or your friends' goals. Take time to think about what you really want, and make them your own. You're more likely to accomplish them if you're personally invested in them.

- Consider what concerns you most. Is there anything that gnaws at your soul and won't let you sleep because you're so worried? Resolving that problem is a high priority for you. Make it a goal, and establish a strategy to accomplish it.

- Find someone who inspires you. I love the story of Jim Ryan, the first man to break the four-minute mile. Most people thought running a mile in less than four minutes was impossible, but Ryan was determined to prove them wrong. His autobiography, *In Quest of Gold*, tells how he set that goal and accomplished it in spite of long odds. Ryan is an inspiration to me and to anyone who has been told that we can't achieve our dreams.

---

16 Brian Tracy, *Goals!*, (Berrett-Koehler Publishers, San Francisco, 2003), p. 50.

- Crystallize your thinking. Some people benefit from imagining a scenario that forces them to think more clearly. For instance, imagine that you just found out that you have a terminal disease and you have only six months to live. What would your goals be? Or think about what it would be like to enjoy your 90th birthday party. Where will you have the party? Describe the details of that party. Who would be there? What will they be saying about you, and what do you want them to say about you?

- Prioritize. All goals aren't equally important, and each of the four types of people (buried in debt, etc.) will have different specific goals, at least for the short-term. Be disciplined and determined to focus on the most important goals first.

- Reexamine your goals from time to time. Things change. Births, deaths, graduations, weddings, promotions, hurricanes, floods, fires, illnesses, injuries, and other major events can affect your goals. Don't be too rigid, but learn to be flexible to tailor your goals to fit your current situation.

Identify your goals and prioritize them to be sure you accomplish what matters most to you.

Identify your goals and prioritize them to be sure you accomplish what matters most to you. Each goal will need a specific date and the funding required. For example, your goals might include:

- college education for your children
- a nice wedding for your daughter
- meaningful vacations for your family
- paying off the mortgage on your home
- a comfortable retirement; for instance, to retire on your birthday, April 15, 2027 with $100,000 in annual income (in today's dollars)
- starting a business
- caring for an elderly parent or a disabled spouse or child

John and Krista had already identified their goals, but they wrestled with the projected amounts and dates when they would need the money. In their calculations, they figured that Krista would go back to work after Angela, their younger child, finished high school. Their goals are:

- College expenses for Jason
  Amount needed for a state university: $80,000
  Beginning: August 2021

- College expenses for Angela
  Amount needed for a state university: $80,000
  Beginning: August 2023

- Wedding for Angela
  Amount needed: $35,000
  Date needed: about 2027

- Family vacations
  Amounts needed: an average of $3000/year
  Dates needed: yearly

- Retirement
  Amount needed: $150,000/year (adjusted for inflation)
  Date needed: beginning on John's 65th birthday, March 22, 2041

John and Krista determined that their top priorities are college expenses for the children and meaningful family vacations.

What are your most important financial goals?
- Goal #1:

  Specific date:
  Dollar amount:

- Goal #2:

    Specific date:
    Dollar amount:

- Goal #3:

    Specific date:
    Dollar amount:

- Goal #4:

    Specific date:
    Dollar amount:

Look at your goals very carefully. List these in order of priority.

    1.

    2.

    3.

    4.

PART 4: ACHIEVING YOUR FINANCIAL GOALS

Look at each of the goals you have prioritized. Describe the sense of fulfillment you'll experience when you accomplish each of these.

ESSENTIAL ELEMENTS OF A FINANCIAL STRATEGY

In the next chapter, we'll examine these elements in more detail and provide worksheets, but we want to introduce them here. A successful financial strategy incorporates several key components, and the final strategy will contain solutions, including specific products and time horizons.

The goal of this section is to help you learn to think like a skilled financial planner. These

> *The goal of this section is to help you learn to think like a skilled financial planner.*

essential elements will give you a firm grasp of the issues involved in developing your strategy.

Financial freedom (or retirement)

Some people want to work the rest of their lives, but others eagerly anticipate retirement so they can travel and devote more time to hobbies, their families, and some important causes. After he retired, my friend Buck transitioned from full-time employment to serving as one of the leaders of our church's men's ministry. His definition of retirement is simple: "It's when I stopped working for money, and money started working for me."

Whether you actually quit work, continue working, or change vocations to become a full-time volunteer, you need a clear plan to achieve financial freedom and accomplish your dreams. Buck paid close attention to his plan, and his plan continues to pay big dividends today.

Some people fear the prospect of retirement because they've heard reports of the impending collapse of Social Security and the rising costs of long-term care and Medicare. Certainly, we need to be aware of the government's policies, but we'd be wise to spend our energies in planning instead of worrying.

Risk management

We deal with many risks, ranging from minor car accidents to catastrophic injury or death. All of us need adequate property and casualty insurance, as well as life insurance. In addition, we need to consider other ways to lower our risk. Experiences of long-term illnesses and disability can cause severe financial hardships, and they can be a burden on those we love. Some of the pain can be alleviated with properly planned insurance.

Education planning

It is important to start putting money aside for college as early as possible. There are many options, each with specific features.

Education planning can be challenging because of the complexities of tax considerations, management fees, parental income limitations, and other issues. For example, some accounts charge a penalty if the money isn't used for college costs. Saving money, borrowing money, and financial aid are some obvious ways to pay for college. As you plan, remember that the inflation rate for college expenses is higher than the rate for other goods and services.

Your overall financial strategy should include a wide range of solutions that insure your children will be able to attend college to achieve their dreams.

Estate planning

Estate planning is a process that determines how to distribute your property during your life and at your death according to your goals and objectives. Without advance planning, more of your assets may go to the federal government in taxes instead of going to the people you love.

The issues that will affect your estate include taxes, probate, liquidity, and incapacity. Your strategy can consist of solutions that are simple and inexpensive (e.g., a will or life insurance). If your estate is large the process can be complex and expensive, and it's wise to involve professionals in estate planning. Even modest portfolios, however, can grow into large ones if they are managed properly, so every person needs to consider estate planning, either now or in the future.

Tax planning

The goal of tax planning is to minimize federal income tax liability while maximizing the after-tax return on investments. Typically, deferring some income in a 401k, 403b, deductible IRA, or other tax-advantaged accounts reduces taxable income. Roth IRA's are excellent vehicles for many Americans to save for tax-free income.

Each person's tax planning strategy is based on individual income and should include solutions that defer taxes and offer tax-free growth whenever possible. Some individuals need expert tax advice in order to design the best strategy, but standard solutions work well for most people.

Investment planning

Almost limitless choices are available to every investor. Your strategy must be designed to get the highest return within your tolerance for risk and your time horizon. No one can guarantee a profit or protect against a loss in a declining market, but diversification limits risk, and dollar cost averaging (using automatic deductions) takes some of the guesswork out of investing. Asset allocation is the most important step in diversifying your portfolio. You can balance risk and return by spreading your dollars among different types of assets, such as stocks, bonds, and cash equivalents. Different types of assets carry different levels of risk and potential for return, and these investment vehicles typically don't respond to market forces in the same way at the same time.

> *Asset allocation is the most important step in diversifying your portfolio.*

A long-term strategy will help you ride out the ups and downs of the market to build a sizeable investment account over your time horizon.

Cash flow

Cash flow (or budgeting) is a process to measure, plan, and prioritize your spending and saving. Your commitment to financial success requires a clear strategy for managing all aspects of your income and expenses. An analysis of cash flow is the starting point in any financial strategy.

Analyze your current financial position honestly and realistically, clarify your goals, and develop a clear financial strategy. On an annual basis, measure your progress.

Working with a Professional

When Rafe and Liz decided to build their house, they knew they didn't have the expertise to design it and build it themselves.

That's why they hired an architect and builder. In the same way, few of us have the savvy to design our own comprehensive financial plans. We may need some assistance and guidance from a professional to help us make the best decisions so that our dreams and goals are fulfilled.

Many of the calculations that seem overwhelming to you are the stock-in-trade of financial professionals. Your role is to clarify the vision and have a firm intention to fulfill your goals; the professional's role is to provide the technical means. For reasons we'll examine in a later chapter, some people don't see financial professionals as trusted resources. That's too bad, because a good professional may help you identify and prioritize your goals, and they may provide valuable insights about choosing the best investments to achieve your goals more quickly and with less stress.[17]

"We brought all this from our previous financial advisor."

SOLOMON'S ADVICE ON FINANCIAL PLANNING

King Solomon was the classic example of someone who had bucks in the bank, but without peace. He ruled the nation, and he commanded the army. He had fabulous wealth, and he indulged

---

17 If you don't know how to find a competent financial professional, go to www.poweredbypurpose.com for more information.

himself on parties, infinite sex, palatial homes, and possessions beyond counting. But all the wealth and pleasure in the world couldn't fill the hole in his heart. He complained, "I've been king over Israel in Jerusalem. I looked most carefully into everything, searched out all that is done on this earth. And let me tell you, there's not much to write home about. God hasn't made it easy for us. I've seen it all and it's nothing but smoke—smoke, and spitting into the wind" (Ecclesiastes 1:12-14). Even though he was disillusioned, God gave him wisdom to understand how life is supposed to work.

My friend Matt Chandler is the lead pastor of The Village Church in Flower Mound, Texas. My wife and I love to listen to his messages.[18] In a study of Ecclesiastes, Matt painted a vivid portrait of King Solomon's lifestyle of rampant consumption. At the end of Solomon's grand, self-indulgent experiment, he warned that everything in life is meaningless without God. But life doesn't have to be that way. Matt challenged people to develop "a sixth sense" in following Jesus to a rich, meaningful life. Matt explained, "When our lives are directed by a transcendent purpose, money can just be money. It no longer becomes our master, and we don't have to have it to gain some kind of social status. We can give money away or buy a house, and it doesn't own us. Christ removes futility and vanity from our souls and gives us the purpose you and I are dying for. Everything else under the sun is running on a treadmill. My hope is that you'll honestly evaluate life, and you'll begin to look beyond the Sun. And I hope you and I develop—even more fully—the sixth sense of faith in Jesus Christ."

The complexity of today's financial vehicles may be a recent phenomenon, but the need for good planning is as old as civilization. Jesus had more to say about money than almost any other subject. In fact, a third of his parables focused on how people handle money. Why is money so important to God? Because the way we use money reveals what's in our hearts, and our courageous choices about money shape the direction of our lives. Solomon wrote about the importance of planning almost a millennia before

---

18   Matt's podcasts are free through itunes or at his website: http://www.thevillagechurch.net/resources/sermons.html

Jesus. He wrote, "Careful planning puts you ahead in the long run; hurry and scurry puts you further behind" (Proverb 21:5).

One of the chief problems, Solomon observed, is that some people are just too lazy to plan. Perhaps they think someone else will take care of them, or they don't see the benefit of spending a little time to provide resources for the people they love, or maybe they haven't determined what matters most to them so they aren't motivated to do the little bit of work necessary for large gains. Whatever the reason, the king noted, "[Laziness] makes you poor; diligence brings wealth. Make hay while the sun shines—that's smart; go fishing during harvest—that's stupid" (Proverbs 10:4-5).

We are wise, Solomon tells us, if we take a hard look at our current condition so we can see immediate or delayed danger. Only the foolish close their eyes to these realities. He encouraged us, "A prudent person sees trouble coming and ducks; a simpleton walks in blindly and is clobbered. The payoff for meekness and Fear-of-God is plenty and honor and a satisfying life" (Proverbs 22:3-4).

"Plenty and honor and a satisfying life." That's Solomon's promise for those who plan for the future. Sure, it takes some time and effort, but the lack of planning produces worry that absorbs our time and depletes our energy. The king encourages us to be smart, not stupid, and to work on our financial plans.

A life of faith is an adventure. Sometimes, we have to make hard decisions, and it seems that God is a million miles away. But at other times, we see him provide for us and lead us very clearly. The more we grasp God's greatness and goodness, the more we'll trust him—even when we don't sense his presence. As we trust him, we'll worry far less. In his most famous talk, Jesus told us that God provides for us in incredible ways. He said, "That is why I tell you not to worry about everyday life—whether you have enough food and drink, or enough clothes to wear. Isn't life more than food, and your body more than clothing? Look at the birds. They don't plant or harvest or store food in barns, for your heavenly Father feeds them. And aren't you far more valuable to him than they are? Can all your worries add a single moment to your life?" (Matthew 6:25-27).

THINK ABOUT IT...

1. Were you able to calculate and write down your total net worth? If so, were you encouraged or disheartened by the reality of that number? Explain your answer. If you couldn't complete this section now, will you commit to taking the time to calculate your net worth in the next 30 days?

2. Are your goals clear or vague at this point? How will it affect you (your attitude, relationships, confidence, etc.) when you have clear financial goals and a powerful strategy to achieve them?

3. In the next chapter, we'll examine the elements of a financial strategy, but as you read the brief descriptions of them in this chapter, which ones seem most important to your goals? Explain your answer.

4. Would the services of a financial planning professional help you? Why or why not?

Going deeper

1. Read Proverbs 21:5, 10:4-5, and 22:3-4. On a scale of 0 (stupid, a simpleton) to 10 (smart, prudent, a careful planner), rate your financial planning abilities up to this moment in your life. Explain your answer.

2. Rate your motivation from 0 to 10 to create an effective financial plan. Do you really believe that having an effective plan will result in "plenty and honor and a satisfying life"? Why or why not?

3. Read Matthew 6:25-27. How would it affect your attitude (thankfulness, peace, etc.) if you really believed that God will provide for you? In light of this passage, what's your part and what's God's part in your financial planning and strategy?

4. If you had only six months to live, what would your priorities be? How could you use your resources to accomplish those priorities?

5 | PUTTING IT ALL TOGETHER

"Everybody's got plans . . . until they get hit." —Mike Tyson

In my work with State Farm, I served as an adjuster on thousands of claims in disasters like the Northridge Earthquake in Los Angeles and Hurricanes Hugo and Andrew. My first experience as a Disaster Adjuster was in the upscale Denver suburb of Cherry Hills, where baseball sized hail splintered wood roofs and shattered windows. Immediately, I noticed that most wealthy people (those who had managed their money wisely) examine every dollar of their claims. With them, handling money wasn't hit or miss.

Years later, I coached a team of independent adjusters following Hurricane Katrina. As I met with people in coastal Alabama, Louisiana, and Mississippi, I learned some valuable lessons. In some catastrophes, such as tornadoes, one family's home is blown away while a neighbor's is left unscathed. But standing on the sand-strewn streets in the towns of southern Mississippi, I saw that everybody's house or business was blown or washed away. Homeowners and business owners were all facing similar circumstances, but people's responses were as different as night and day. In New Orleans, the devastation was so widespread that the future of entire communities was at risk.

Sam and Kim owned and operated a fast-food restaurant in a hard hit part of New Orleans. When we paid their claim, they had

117

enough money to replace their facility or move to a more profitable location. They decided to rebuild in the same location as quickly as possible in order to provide free food for less fortunate people in their community. Sam and Kim had no doubt that they would eventually regain financial stability, but during the difficult aftermath of Hurricane Katrina, they had other priorities. They weren't alone in their care for others. Gripping stories of true heroes, who risked their lives to rescue stressed and stranded people, filled newspapers and television screens across the globe. Meanwhile, refugees who had been displaced by the storm were being relocated around the country. Many of them came to Houston where our generous city opened the Astrodome and other city-owned facilities to provide food and shelter. Churches, synagogues, and even individual homes were opened to provide support for our neighbors from New Orleans. My family and many of our friends had firsthand experience helping people who were humble and thankful for so many acts of kindness.

In sharp contrast to this gratitude, several young people from New Orleans were offered homemade sandwiches and soft drinks provided by a local church congregation. They refused the offer, demanding beer and McDonald's hamburgers instead. Sadly, this example isn't an isolated one. I helped a man with his claim, but he was so stressed that he threatened to kill me if I didn't pay him more than his policy limit.

Soon, it became obvious that thankful people are heroes who face adversity with courage and concern for others.

As I watched both kinds of people—the thankful and the demanding—I asked myself, *What's the difference?* Soon, it became obvious that thankful people are heroes who face adversity with courage and concern for others. They're governed by a mysterious and powerful blend of faith, hope, and love.

None of us are masters of the universe who can avoid life's catastrophic curveballs like Hurricane Katrina. No amount of insurance or investment planning can completely protect us from these forms of devastation. However, sound financial planning provides stability and strength to enable us to offer a hand to others who may not have planned so well.

Financial planning may seem strange at first, but it's not rocket science. The principles are clear and straightforward, and learning them requires only a modest investment of time. This chapter addresses seven essential elements of financial planning that are like pieces of a puzzle. When we put them together, they form our financial strategy and give us confidence in the future. We glanced at them in the last chapter, but we'll explore them a bit more in this one. The acronym of these elements is FREETIC. To help you remember this word, I asked an artist friend to draw a "free tick" for us.[19]

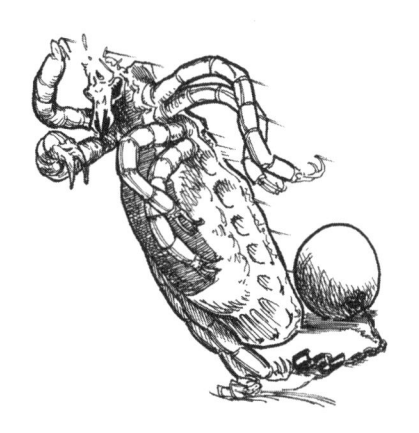

FINANCIAL FREEDOM

I've known a lot of people who lived to work and poured their lives into a company. Soon after they got gold watches at their retirement parties, however, the people at the party were attending their funerals. Without meaningful work and a sense of purpose, their lives simply ended. Life is much more than a career. Your purpose in life can transcend your work and give everything—including your work—far more meaning.

Jack and Natalie have done it right. Jack worked long and hard for a global company in the construction business, and he looked forward to retirement. But after Jack's last day at work, he and Natalie didn't plan on just taking a deep breath and becoming self-absorbed for the rest of their lives. Years ago, they began pouring their lives into other people: their kids, their church, and their work

---

19   For worksheets on each of these elements, talk to your financial planning professional or go to www.poweredbypurpose.com.

with Habitat for Humanity. After a few wild and wooly years when they were young, Jack and Natalie figured out that their friends' version of "having it all" often meant having nothing that matters. So, they woke up and made some decisions to go in a different direction. They found Christ, or as Natalie would tell you, Christ found them, and their lives have never been the same. As they spent time with people who cared about others and made wise choices, Jack and Natalie absorbed those values, too.

Many years before Jack got his gold watch, he and Natalie began to connect their time and money to the things that mattered most to them. When he retired, Jack had more time to spend helping other people. When they talk about their work at church and with Habitat, their eyes light up. Their example hasn't been lost on their kids, either. Both of them are known for their delight in helping others.

The purpose of planning for retirement is simply to have options when we get to that point in our lives. I don't think retirement is meant to enable us to stop doing things that are constructive and useful. That sounds more like death to me. If we plan and invest wisely, we'll have the opportunity to invest our lives in whatever we choose. Some may feel so fulfilled at work that they never want to leave, some may change jobs and do something they've always dreamed of trying, and some may become full-time volunteers (with a little more golf thrown in from time to time) for an organization that's doing something that thrills their souls. Doing nothing, though, isn't a good option.

If we plan and invest wisely, we'll have the opportunity to invest our lives in whatever we choose.

The timing of financial independence (a term I like better than retirement) depends on a number of factors, but greater wealth brings a wider range of options earlier in our lives. I know men and women who changed course in their mid-40s to volunteer for a non-profit organization. They had made enough to live on, and they valued their contribution to the organization more than a fatter bottom line. For years, they had given their money to the organization, and now they wanted to give not only their money, but also their lives. They were giving to live.

For a number of reasons, some of us have devoted our lives to corporate America. The benefits of abject loyalty to an employer can be significant financial rewards and accolades, but the cost can be quite steep. Living only to climb the corporate ladder may one day bring the painful realization that our ladder has been leaning against the wrong wall. I'm certainly not saying that corporations are inherently evil. No, not at all. If our purpose in life is to give, love, and serve, then we can fulfill that purpose everywhere we go, but we have to be careful not to let the benefits of corporate America sit on the throne of our lives. Jesus said that we "can't serve God and money." We have to make a choice. One results in life, purpose, and peace; the other results in competition, comparison, and neglect of the things that really matter. We have to clearly define a purpose that grips our hearts, and then we have to draw boundaries around our hearts to protect them and defend them from the lure of money, position, and power.

To achieve financial independence, we first have to want it. Of course, we'd all say we want it, but we have to want it *more than* the immediate gratification that comes from having more stuff now. This desire leads to choices—decisions to invest in the future.

When we have a desire, we need to take action as soon as possible (we'll look at the magic of compound interest in the next chapter). The point is to save as much as you can as early as you can, and if they're offered, take advantage of matching funds by your employer. This way, you instantly double your money, and as compound interest works its magic, you make far more money down the road. I often meet with young people who tell me, "Jim, I'd love to put money in my 401k, but I don't make enough." In most cases (but not all), I notice they drove to my office in a nearly new car, and they're wearing the latest style in clothes. Desire determines choices. In most cases, if they really want to start investing in their futures, they can make adjustments in their spending so they'll have the money to invest.

As I explain the advantages of investing early, many people look at me and say sadly, "I wish I'd started saving and investing earlier." We can't turn back the clock, but we can make decisions today to invest as *much* as we can, as *soon* as we can, as *consistently* as we can.

RISK MANAGEMENT

Most people have property and casualty insurance on their homes, cars, or business, but a lot of people don't have *adequate* insurance. In my work following Hurricane Katrina, I met lots of successful people who had devoted their time and energies to growing their businesses or serving their organizations, but they hadn't carved out 15 minutes to review their insurance policies to keep them updated. It broke my heart to see the looks on people's faces when they realized that their coverage wasn't what they thought it was. They had assumed that all insurance is the same, but that's simply not the case. Some were grossly underinsured, and they'll spend the rest of their lives suffering financially. Fifteen minutes invested with their agents could have made a world of difference for these individuals and their families, and for business owners and their companies.

As I've traveled across the country working on disaster relief, I've learned that a lot of agents haven't helped their clients update their coverage and get the best value for their insurance dollar. Some of the biggest accounts in my insurance agency have come because a business owner called and told me, "I've asked my agent three times to meet with me to update my policies, but he hasn't been in the office. Will you come and look at my property to make sure I'm covered, Jim?" It's important to update your property and

It's important to update your property and casualty coverage regularly, every year or every other year, to make sure you're getting the best value and all available discounts.

casualty coverage regularly, every year or every other year, to make sure you're getting the best value and all available discounts. Your agent may be able to save you a good deal of money, or she may suggest another policy to protect your assets. My advice is to plan on investing 30 minutes a year with your agent. If the experience is too painful, find another agent who makes the process more pleasant, but don't expect a miracle *after* the disaster from an agent who has no clue what matters most to you *before* the disaster.

When most people think of risk management, they instantly think of car and home insurance. But three other areas are vitally important:

Life insurance

I've seen both sides. When an uncle died recently, he neglected to leave a will or any life insurance, so the family was strapped—financially and emotionally—paying for the funeral and settling his meager estate. On the other hand, when Connie's father was murdered, he had two life insurance policies that helped the family cope with those dark days. The policeman who investigated his death was Gail Joslin. At the time, I was considering becoming a policeman, but Gail told me, "The only reason I stay in this job is that it pays my life insurance. I have diabetes, and I don't qualify for life insurance. I'd love to do something else, but I can't." Similarly, I've known someone whose company was downsized. When he was laid off, his poor health prevented him from getting insurance (and the cheap company insurance was no longer cheap). In both cases, Gail's point is well taken: If you're healthy, own your own life insurance policy. You'll have more control of your financial future, and you won't be locked into a job you don't enjoy.

If part of what matters most is your family, you need to leave them with financial stability when you die. To neglect that responsibility wounds them and clouds your legacy. Several types of life insurance are available, and the factors of each person's case determine the best course. Most experts say that cash value life insurance is a waste of money, but I can give you names and phone numbers of lots of people who found it to be the very best option for them.

Term life insurance is inexpensive and the best solution for most people, but it's temporary.

Always check out the insurance company to be sure it is reputable and can pay the claim. Find out how many policies they have in force and their level of assets. You can check out any company online or with your agent. A little homework will save a huge headache for you or for those you love. Be sure you know how much the policy will cost you down the road, when you're 50, 60, or 90. Term life insurance is cheap when you're young and healthy, but the cost increases with age and any health problems. Will you need it when you are older, or will your investments provide financial freedom for your family? If you need it when you're older, will you be able to afford the higher cost? Will you be healthy enough to qualify for a policy? Remember to think ahead. You'll probably be on a fixed income later in your life when your premiums will be extremely high. It might be wise to buy a permanent (cash value) policy that stays the same price for your "whole life." Yes, I know, the experts will tell you a whole life policy is a poor investment. They're right: As an investment, it's a poor choice, but it may be a great way to protect your family if you haven't gotten around to building a nest egg or if you have to spend your savings for an unexpected expense.

Disability insurance

When I was an agent in Pennsylvania, I had a client named Don who used to go to the auto races. One day he was sitting on a knoll above the stands. He reached down to pick up his beer, and at that moment, a tire came off a car and careened up the hill. Others had been watching and jumped out of the way, but Don didn't see it coming. It hit him squarely in the chest and face, crushing bones in both places. He died on the scene, but he was resuscitated on the way to the hospital. Reconstructive surgery put him back together, but months later, he still wasn't back at work. One day when I visited him, he told me with a tear in his eye, "Jim, I'm so grateful you advised me to get disability insurance. I don't know what would have happened to my family all these months without it."

Disability insurance is often overlooked, but statistics show that 1 person in 5 will be disabled at some point. This insurance is relatively inexpensive, and it can make a world of difference to the family of someone who misses paychecks for an extended period.

Long-term care

People are living longer, but not necessarily better. The science of medicine is keeping older people alive, but at some point, many of them will be unable to live on their own. Today, the parents of several friends of mine are in nursing homes and other long-term care facilities. A few of them made preparations—most didn't. Those facilities are expensive, and some of my friends face mounting bills they had no idea they'd have to pay. Other friends and clients have chosen to rearrange their lives and careers so that they could provide care for a lingering loved one in their own homes. Long-term care will be one of the biggest financial hurdles many families face in the coming years, and some will face it at the same time their children go to college and get married.

> *Long-term care will be one of the biggest financial hurdles many families face in the coming years.*

To be sure, not every person needs long-term care insurance, but I believe everybody needs to at least have an honest conversation about it.

EDUCATION PLANNING

In many families, the parents own the vision for their children's education, but for some reason, they don't impart that vision to the kids. When only the parents are passionate about their children's college degrees, kids often feel pushed. At that age, adolescents try to carve out their own identities, and when they feel pushed, they either become resistant or passive, which is a long way from a clear vision for the future enflaming their passion for education!

I encourage parents to start early, when their kids are in grade school, to talk about the importance of college. A college degree certainly doesn't guarantee success, but it opens a lot of doors that remain closed to those with only a high school diploma. As the gifts and talents of each child surface in middle school and high school, parents can talk more about the merits of different colleges and universities. They can talk honestly and openly about the costs of those schools, especially the difference in cost between public and private universities. Parents and their kids may need to compromise to make things work. For instance, a friend of mine told his two children he had set aside enough money for both of them to attend a state school. One of them chose that path, but the other had different dreams. He wanted to attend college in California, so he and his parents calculated that he could attend a local junior college for two years and then transfer to a private school across the country for the remaining two years. His father realized that this compromise would bump up against the limits of his funds, so he told his son before he started college, "This can work, but you'll need to work during the two years you're in junior college to pay for your gas, entertainment, and other expenses. When you walk out the door to go to the private school, you have to have at least $3000 in your savings account." This arrangement motivated the young man, and he worked hard in school and in a job before he left. On the day he left home, he had $3025 in his account, and he excelled in his college career.

One of the most overlooked resources for college funding is financial aid. Colleges and universities offer a wide array of merit-based and need-based grants, loans, and scholarships. Many parents, however, fail to take advantage of them. Perhaps one reason students drag their feet is that they often have to write an essay to apply for the funds. They don't want to have to do another paper in high school, even if this one might bring in a lot of dollars. If the parents haven't talked openly about their financial limitations, their kids might not be motivated to pursue these avenues simply because they don't have a vision for their own education.

A financial planning professional can help you explore all the opportunities available, but don't forget to start talking with your children years before they're ready to walk out the door to go to college. Model a life of purpose by focusing on what matters most, and help them develop a vision for their lives so they'll take ownership of their plans for college.

In some cases, high school students have far more vision for the future than their parents. Not long ago, a young man who is a junior in high school called me for an appointment. His parents are deeply in debt, and they have no money for his college education. That reality, he was determined, wouldn't stop him. He told me, "Mr. Munchbach, I know my parents can't pay for college, so I'm here today to talk to you about what I need to do. Can you help me?"

We had an amazing conversation. His maturity and vision thrilled me, and I listened intently as he told me about his vision for his future. I have some contacts at a local university, so I called the Dean of Admissions to schedule an appointment for this young man. He took a battery of tests, and the next day, the Dean called me. He said, "Jim, I've never seen a student like this before. He is so motivated to go to college. In most cases, I do assessments and then have difficulty finding the students to give them the results. He just took the tests yesterday, and he has already called me! His vision for his life is amazing."

Estate Planning

I could say that I'm astounded that so many seemingly responsible men and women have neglected to draw a will, but that would be hypocritical because Connie and I delayed having ours drawn for many years. From time to time, the need to have one would surface, but I always found an excuse to put it off. As I look back on our procrastination, it seems ridiculous.

If we genuinely care about our families, we'll leave a will with clear instructions about what to do with the stuff we leave behind. All of us know horror stories of families torn apart because the deceased person left no will or an unclear one. We can save those we love from the pain and bitterness that can be unleashed when greed rears its ugly head. And in fact, directions about the stuff we leave behind may not be the most important feature in our wills. We can use this opportunity to express heartfelt appreciation and love for each member of our family, and we can explain why we are leaving grandmother's bed to our son and the gold necklace to our daughter. We can also use the will to give specific instructions about the use and limits of funds. For example, some of my clients include a clause in their wills that if they die before their children graduate from college, the money will go into a trust until graduation.

Today, some people are using the latest technology to express their love and to explain the reasons they made the decisions reflected in their wills. Audio and video give us an opportunity to express our love one more time, or to say things we've always wanted to say.

It takes only about 15 minutes to go online, search for a service to help write a simple will, and provide the basic information. The cost is minimal. If you want to designate more things to specific people and to express your reasons or the history of each piece, you'll be motivated to spend a little more time to make sure you communicate clearly.

All of us need to consider specific issues in estate planning such as taxes, probate, the selection of the executor, and liquidity of funds, but those with a large estate may have a more complicated situation requiring professional help. Whether your will is simple or complex, review it regularly—at least every five years or when circumstances (marriage, death of a spouse, change in finances) necessitate a second look.

Leaving this life without a will can devastate those left behind, and it leaves a legacy that doesn't honor our memory.

Leaving this life without a will can devastate those left behind, and it leaves a legacy that doesn't honor our memory. I've mentioned an uncle who died without a will. The family is still struggling with the financial and emotional impact of his neglect.

When Elvis Presley died, his estate was valued at over $10 million, but he hadn't done any estate planning to lower his estate tax (also known as a "death tax"), so the estate of the "King of Rock and

Roll" paid $7 million to the IRS. Singer James Brown's will begins: "I, James Brown, also known as 'The Godfather of Soul.' " Brown died with a will naming his six children as heirs, but it excludes "any other relatives or persons whether claiming, or claim to be an heir of mine or not." Brown's will did not mention his "life partner" Tomi Rae Hynie or their 5-year-old son. She and their son will have to sue in order to inherit any of the estate. Similarly, Anna Nicole Smith's death was a media circus and a legal disaster. An updated will easily could have specified the care and custody of her baby daughter, Dannielynn. Celebrities like these—and the rest of us—can minimize pain, confusion, and conflict for the people we leave behind by following a few simple estate-planning tips before we die.

In our culture, many of us avoid thoughts about death at all cost, but this perspective misses some of life's most important lessons. King Solomon observed, "You learn more at a funeral than at a feast—After all, that's where we'll end up. We might discover something from it" (Ecclesiastes 7:2). Thinking about death has multiple benefits: We learn to treasure each moment and each person in this life, and we're motivated to leave a legacy of love and hope.

Tax Planning

In *The Millionaire Next Door,* authors Thomas Stanley and William Danko studied the habits, values, and lifestyles of millionaires, and they found that many of them give focused attention to tax planning to minimize their tax liability. They use every available resource: 401k or 403b, deductible IRA, Roth IRA, and other accounts with tax advantages. Saving money on taxes is choice, low hanging fruit. It may seem complicated, but it's actually very simple. All of us can learn a few things, make a few choices, and save a significant amount of money.

A couple of years ago, a man came to my office to prepare for retirement, but he already had a clear vision and strategy. He showed me his list of assets, and I asked him how he had accumulated so much money. He replied, "Jim, my plan was to take full advantage of every single opportunity offered by the IRS." He simply wanted me to help him maximize the assets he had accumulated in his 401k and his Roth IRA. He came to me for advice, but I learned a lot from him that day. His plan is very simple, but it proved to be quite effective. By paying himself first (in his 401k plan), he paid the IRS less and paid himself more. Now he's a millionaire.

Those of us with modest income and assets can use one of the tax prep software packages, but people with significant resources usually enlist the help of an accountant. In fact, Stanley and Danko found that the most trusted financial advisor for millionaires is their accountant.

Recently, I talked to two accountants and asked them why their clients come to them. They both said exactly the same thing: "My clients hate surprises." The goal of each client is to pay as little and keep as much as possible, but they don't like to ever hear, "Unfortunately, you have a big tax bill this year." When it's time to send in the 1040, it's too late to do anything about the past year. Tax planning must occur early enough to make a difference. Rich people get rich by paying close attention to every penny. Lucrative investments bring in a lot of money, but tax planning helps close the back door so less goes out.

INVESTMENTS

When people use the term "financial planning," many people think only about investments. But investments are only one of the seven pieces of the puzzle. I explain to my clients that they can consider three types of accounts, which I call three "buckets":

- The gold bucket contains tax-free instruments like the Roth IRA. This has the most potential for tax savings and significant income in the future.

- The silver bucket includes instruments that are tax deductible, like 401k, a 403b, or a traditional IRA. With these, we get a deduction today, and we defer taxes until later when we withdraw funds from the accounts.

- The bronze bucket contains a wide array of accounts, such as stocks, bonds, and real estate, for which we pay taxes before we invest and on income realized from the investments.

The world's foremost investor, Warren Buffett, commented, "Investing is not like Olympic diving. You don't get extra points for difficulty." The fundamentals of investing aren't difficult to grasp, but they provide a wealth of wisdom about how to allocate our funds for maximum return and security. Three important principles are diversification, asset allocation, and dollar cost averaging. Let me explain these concepts:

Diversification

Only a few years ago, the collapse of Enron dominated the business news, but for some people I know, the national news was painfully personal. In the years just prior to the company's collapse, the company urged employees to keep all their retirement funds in Enron stock. One of my clients realized that was a risk she wasn't willing to take, but another client bought the company's promises of long-term stability. Beth came to me a few months after the company filed bankruptcy. For all intents and purposes, Enron had ceased to exist, but she had a huge amount of money to invest. I asked, "How did you get out of there with all this money?"

She replied, "I saw the writing on the wall, so I took my money out of Enron stock well before it tanked, and I put it in other funds." Today, Beth's retirement account is doing quite well.

But Frank didn't see the writing on the wall. He believed the officers who told him, "Don't worry. Everything will be just fine." In the heyday of the company, Frank had over $1 million in Enron stock in his retirement account. A few months later, he had nothing. The financial setback was too much for him. The pain and shame caused panic attacks, then a heart attack. Frank died as another casualty of Enron's financial mismanagement.

Diversification is a way to spread risk so the problem Frank experienced doesn't happen to you. My favorite illustration comes from my friend David Coney at Edward Jones. David taught me to illustrate diversification by talking about elevators. I tell the client he has a choice of two elevators. A single cable holds up one elevator, and eight strong cables hold the other. The building, I tell the client, is 100 years old.

Then I ask, "Which elevator would you take to the top floor?"

This question often elicits a chuckle and a quick reply, "The one with lots of cables."

The single cable may be strong for a long time, but if and when it ever breaks, people in the elevator will be in trouble. But if one of the eight cables on the other one breaks, the other cables can hold it very securely. This simple drawing illustrates the difference between trusting in one financial product (that is, "putting all your eggs in one basket") and having a diverse portfolio. This illustration also describes the benefits of mutual funds over individual stocks. In these funds, managers check the cables (individual stocks) in their diversified holdings, and replace those that aren't performing well or have too much risk.

It's sound, established, financial logic to avoid having too many assets in a single investment, but some executives, managers, and employees view their company's stock like it's their first-born child. For example, one man told me, "I'd never sell my company's stock. I'd feel disloyal." We talked further about the benefits of diversifying, and ultimately, logic prevailed. Some people, however, won't budge. Their emotional investment in their pet stock is so strong that they simply can't bring themselves to sell any portion of it.

Asset allocation

The distribution of assets to balance risk and reward is the most important principle of investing. A little wisdom makes a huge difference in the return on investment. A lady named Kimberly came to me, and she was visibly upset. Her husband Ed had an IRA with $100,000, but he had kept it in a money market at .5% during five years the market had gained 10 to 16% each year. They were both about 35 years old. Dozens of times, she had suggested that he move his money to more productive instruments, and finally, he agreed to meet with me. I explained asset allocation, and they both felt much more comfortable about investing the money. They understood inflation was a big risk to their future, but properly allocating their assets in the market would help them balance risk and return. When I showed them the math, they were stunned. Here's what I explained: If they kept that $100,000 in the money market (cash) account at .5% from age 35 to age 65, the account would be worth only $116,140. By investing their 401k into a diversified family of mutual funds with an expected return of 8% compounded annually, the amount would jump to $1,006,265! Kimberley and Ed almost fought each other to see who would sign the papers to move the funds.

Asset allocation needs to factor in these elements:
- Your risk tolerance, which determines how aggressive or conservative your investments will be,
- The time horizon for achieving your stated goals, such as college education for a child in 2 years and retirement in 35 years, and
- The market dynamics of cash, bonds, equities, and real estate and their relationship to one another to maximize returns while minimizing risk.

Three factors determine the performance of your portfolio: asset allocation, the selection of assets, and market timing. In a ten-year study of ninety-one large corporate pension plans in the United States, the authors of an article in *Financial Analysts Journal* found that 94% of performance was determined by asset allocation. Investment selection accounted for 4%, and market timing was responsible for only 2%.[20]

The metaphor I use to explain asset allocation is balancing a tire. When I was a mechanic, and a customer came to my shop because the car was shaking, the problem was almost always that a tire was out of balance, sometimes caused by a small bump of rubber from uneven wear. Even a seemingly small imbalance of a quarter of an ounce could cause the tire to shake violently at high speeds. I applied a weight to counterbalance the wheel. We checked it on the balancing machine to be sure it ran smoothly, put it back on the car, and the customer was ready to go.

Asset allocation balances the portfolio, so the assets run smoothly toward your goals. Sometimes people only need to make small adjustments, but often they need to make major changes in the distribution of assets. Some people are so risk-averse that they want to keep all their money in cash, and they want to divide it up so they stay under the FDIC limits in each institution. But this strategy only limits risk in the immediate future. Returns on cash accounts don't even keep pace with inflation, so there is no opportunity for asset appreciation and they actually increase their long-term risk.

---

20 B.G.P. Brinson, B.D. Singer, and G.I. Beebower, "Determinants of Portfolio Performance," *Financial Analysts Journal* (January/February, 1986).

Dollar cost averaging

Many of us are tempted to wait for a windfall—winning the lottery or a big inheritance from Aunt Phoebe—before we even start to invest. Our hopes are high because we've heard stories of people who hit it big, but those stories are in the news because they're so rare, not because they're commonplace. The best way to develop a substantial nest egg is to develop the discipline of putting money into a fund every month—no excuses. The market will go up or down, but our funds continue to grow slowly and steadily. I know people who began putting as little as $25 a month into an investment, and over time, they've accumulated a substantial amount of money. When they were young, they had every reason to put off investing because they could easily use that $25 for dinner and a movie. But they were committed to save and invest, even if it was a small amount. When they got promotions and raises, they increased the amount they put away each month.

To explain the benefit of regular investing, I use the illustration of a farmer who invests each month in his favorite commodity: cattle. Farmer Joe calls me and wants to invest $100 each month. When he begins, the market for cattle is near an all-time high. Cattle sell for $100 each. He wonders if this is the right time to invest, but he needs more cattle. The first month, he can buy only one cow. In the second month, the price of cattle goes down to $50, so he buys two. The third month, the price goes to $25, so he buys four that month. And in the fourth month, the price of cattle plummets to a low: $20 each. At that point he calls me and says, "Hey bucko, what have you gotten me into? Cattle are $20 a head! I bought all these cattle at high prices, and the bottom has dropped out of the market! I'm going to sell them all and cut my losses."

I tell him confidently, "Farmer Joe, the market is very low right now. You were paying $100 a head four months ago. You needed cattle, didn't you? Has that changed? No? So why are you upset? This is the best time to *buy* cattle, not sell. Hang in there. You're in great shape to benefit from this phase of the cycle."

Farmer Joe bites his lip and decides to trust me. The next month, the price creeps up to $25 again. Farmer Joe buys four head. The next month, the price has risen to $50, so he buys two, and the next month, the price of cattle is back up to its high of $100, and he buys only one head. At that point, Farmer Joe decides to sell. During those seven months, he bought nineteen cows for a total of $700. They're worth $1900, yielding a net profit of $1200, and the price of cattle never rose above $100 a head. Farmer Joe's only regret was that he didn't sell his tractor and buy more cattle when they were $20 each.

As I explain this story, I draw a chart for my clients. It looks something like this (except that my cows don't look this good).

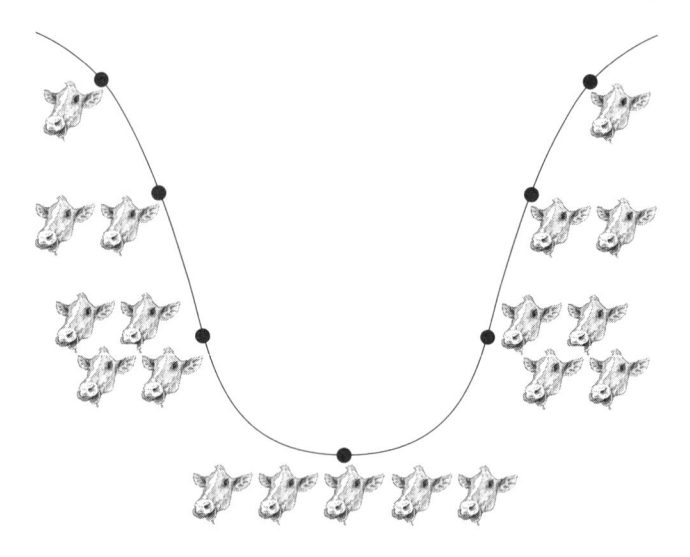

CASH FLOW

When we think about designing a budget, some of us get excited, but many people roll their eyes in boredom. Our cash flow, though, is where vision becomes reality. The choices we make each month about the money in our checking account are directly tied to what matters most. Without a clear purpose and stated financial goals, we'll probably spend money on whatever looks like it will make us happy for the moment. But if we've determined that what matters most is our family's future, our children's college education, and our passion for serving others, then we can gladly make decisions today to allocate funds to achieve those goals.

If we think of our budget as a diet we don't enjoy, we're missing the point. Cash flow isn't a diet of "don'ts" and "can'ts": It's a feast of fulfilling the dreams, desires, and vision for our lives and our families. We can get excited about that!

For those who are buried in debt, the first goal is to get out of debt. When they achieve that goal, they join the rest of us in making decisions to allocate our funds to those things that we've determined are most important. Instead of buying a new car, we're happy to drive our used car another year or two and put the money we're saving into a college fund. Cash flow focuses on decisions that are right now, right here, but the choices are determined by our desires for the future.

The Power of Vision

People who have developed their financial plans and have seen success know that these seven elements provide direction and confidence for their planning. They've clarified their vision, taken the first steps to develop a plan, and allocated their resources in following the plan. And now, they are reaping the rewards. I wish I could introduce you to people you've met in these pages so you'd see their excitement. James and Sheila, Rafe and Liz, Suzanne, Rick Baldwin, and many more have connected their resources to what matters most, and they enjoy that delicious blend of contentment and excitement. They see the seven elements of a financial plan as building blocks of hope, security, and strength.

But for any number of reasons, many others haven't taken these steps. They still see financial planning as a bore, or they feel ashamed that they've failed and they don't want to be reminded of failure again. Whatever the reason, they're missing out on one of the most significant things they can ever do for their own peace of mind and their family's security. Maybe they just need to find a wise friend who will help them take that first step.

Throughout these pages, we've talked often about the thrill of using our resources to touch others lives, beginning with our families and often reaching beyond to touch people in our communities and the world. Part of our vision, then, gives direction to our investment in organizations we believe in. Donations are part of our cash flow.

CONNECT GIVING AND PURPOSE

All of us—Christians, Jews, Muslims, Buddhists, Hindus, agnostics, or whatever we believe or don't believe—have countless opportunities to donate to national or local causes. Sadly, many of us give haphazardly, if at all, without connecting our giving with our purpose in life. I've watched some men and women (and hopefully, I'm becoming one of them) whose resources are closely connected to what matters most to them. They funnel their funds toward building strong family relationships and providing a platform for their children's future, but they also give their time and money to causes that touch them deeply. The Christian writer Fenelon observed, "Small plans do not enflame the hearts of men." Small plans and self-absorbed purposes do not enflame our hearts so that we open our wallets to make a difference in other's lives.

It's at this point that some writers and speakers will tell you where to give your money and how much you should give. I'm not going to do that. I only encourage you to take stock of your giving and take steps to connect your giving to the things that matter to you. If that's the Red Cross, Amnesty International, or a political party, put your whole heart into those organizations and give to their missions. If Christ's love and forgiveness have captured your heart, find a church or an organization that effectively communicates God's message and imparts real life, and give there. My pastor, Rick Baldwin, told our church, "If the ministry of this church doesn't thrill your soul so that you are genuinely excited to support it, don't give. Find a church that you believe in, go there, and give generously."

Many of us give because we become aware of needs in others' lives. Scenes of helpless victims of hurricanes and tsunamis, or the need for a new building for a growing children's ministry, or countless other needs in our communities and the world can touch our hearts and open our pockets. But gratitude is an even stronger and more enduring motivation to give. Throughout the biblical narrative, we see men and women who are so overwhelmed with thankfulness for God's forgiveness and blessings that they gladly give back to him. God enabled Abraham to win a battle and save his family, so Abraham spontaneously gave a tenth of all he owned to God's representative, Melchizedek. When David's men brought the ark back to Jerusalem, he was so thrilled that he danced in the street before he sacrificed offerings to God. Just before Jesus was crucified, Jesus was in Bethany. His friend Mary was so overcome with gratitude for Jesus that she poured expensive perfume on Jesus' feet and wiped his feet with her hair. A poor old woman had only two cents to her name, but she gave it all to God out of love for him.

Needs come and go, but the incomparable riches of God's grace never cease to amaze us. I'm convinced that "growing in Christ" is growing in our awareness of our desperate need for God's grace and our heart-felt appreciation for his overflowing provision of love, kindness, and strength. That's a reason to celebrate, and that's a reason to give.

That's a reason to celebrate, and that's a reason to give.

Some people ask me, "Jim, shouldn't I tithe 10%?" Certainly, the discipline of giving is as important as the discipline of investing, but neither will last long if we aren't convinced that they're worth it. The more important questions are, "Do I really believe in this organization? I don't expect it to be perfect, but do its goals and methods line up with my heart's desire? Do I trust its leaders?" If our hearts are fully engaged, then we'll give as much as we possibly can. In fact, we may have arguments at home because we want to give too much to a cause! Wouldn't that be a hoot?

The first move is to step back, take a look at our hearts and our giving, and assess the clarity of our purpose and the degree our giving thrills us. If we give only because we have to, we won't give much, and we won't receive much joy from writing checks. Recently, I talked with some friends about the reasons people give to a church. Several reasons were listed, but one of my friends said, "Yeah, but I enjoy giving when I have an emotional connection with the cause—if I see myself as a partner in a bigger vision." Exactly. You and I have the privilege of choosing where we allocate our resources, as we invest, save, spend, and give. Everything—every resource we possess—can be connected to the people and causes that enflame our hearts. Don't settle for anything less.

A Solid Foundation

A little planning makes a world of difference. Actually, I'm amazed at how much difference it makes for someone to take some time to clarify what matters most to them and then connect their resources with their goals.

At the end of his most famous message, Jesus talked about two carpenters who tried to build houses on different foundations. He told people, " 'These words I speak to you are not incidental additions to your life, homeowner improvements to your standard of living. They are foundational words, words to build a life on. If you work these words into your life, you are like a smart carpenter who built his house on solid rock. Rain poured down, the river flooded, a tornado hit—but nothing moved that house. It was fixed to the rock. But if you just use my words in Bible studies and don't work them into your life, you are like a stupid carpenter who built his house on the sandy beach. When a storm rolled in and the waves came up, it collapsed like a house of cards.' When Jesus concluded his address, the crowd burst into applause. They had never heard teaching like this. It was apparent that he was living everything he was saying—quite a contrast to their religion teachers! This was the best teaching they had ever heard" (Matthew 7:24-29).

The choice to build on a solid foundation always comes well before the storm.

Earlier in his talk, Jesus taught about his purpose for our lives. He talked about faith, forgiveness, and fairness, and he encouraged us to pursue a life that's full of wisdom. As he concluded his talk, he painted a verbal picture of a choice each of us can make: to build our lives on a solid foundation or try to build it on shifting sand. One results in strength and stability, but the other leads to disaster. The choice to build on a solid foundation always comes well before the storm. For a number of years, I built my house on the sand of wanting to look good in others' eyes, reaching for success at all costs, and filling my life with stuff. And the result was gnawing emptiness and strained relationships with those I love most. At a point years ago, though, I made a different choice to build the rest of my life on the solid foundation of Christ's love, forgiveness, purpose, and power. Jesus' story about the carpenters isn't just about money, but neither is this book. Both are about what really matters in life. When we discover that, we connect everything else to it.

THINK ABOUT IT...

1. What is one insight you learned or were reminded of when you read about:

    —Financial freedom?

    —Risk management?

    —Education?

—Estate planning?

—Tax planning?

—Investments?

—Cash flow?

2. Which of these are areas of strength for you?

3. Which are areas that need some attention?

4. As you think about these seven elements of a financial plan, what are three or four things you need to do soon to get on track?

5. In what way is defining our purpose the first and most important piece of the puzzle as we try to put together a financial strategy?

6. Take stock of your current pattern of donations. To what extent are you thrilled to give to those causes? How much do they enflame your heart? What difference would it make to connect your giving to a cause that you really believe in?

GOING DEEPER

1. Read Matthew 7:24-29. As you think about your purpose in life and the seven elements of a financial strategy, what would it look like to build on a solid foundation?

2. On a sandy one?

6 | Small Steps, Big Payoffs

"I've spent $40,000 on shoes, and I have no place to live!? I will literally be the old woman who lived in her shoes!" —Carrie, Sex and the City, *"Ring a Ding Ding, What's It All Worth?"*

In the last chapter, we looked at seven important components of a financial strategy, but now we want to turn to some principles and practices that have caused a lot of people to say, "Wow! That's incredible!" When we realize the implications of our decisions, we'll see that these are small steps that result in surprisingly big payoffs.

For example, a couple of friends try to eat lunch every day (that they aren't meeting with clients) for less than $2 each. One of them explained, "I certainly don't need to eat a big lunch every day, and besides that, we can have just as good a conversation over a $1.50 burrito as we can over a $10 trout. I don't have all the money in the world, and I want my money to go into things I treasure: trips with my wife and kids. If I save $5 a day five days a week for 52 weeks, that's $1300 I can spend on making memories for all of us. Pretty cool, huh?"

Yes, that's pretty cool. I've noticed that it's kind of a game to these two guys. They aren't obsessed with saving money on lunch, but they're glad to find a good deal!

Here are some insights, principles, and practical suggestions you might want to try.

THE MAGIC OF COMPOUND INTEREST

The impact of compound interest is perhaps the most significant factor in accumulating wealth. It doesn't take a genius to understand it and use it. For instance, if a 20 year old puts $2000 a year for only 10 years into an IRA at 8% and never puts another dime into it, he'll have over $1 million when he's 65. But if his buddy waits until he's 30 to begin and continues to put $2000 a year into the fund for 35 years until he's 65, he won't catch up to his early-bird friend.

The impact of compound interest is perhaps the most significant factor in accumulating wealth.

In these pages, I've mentioned the advantage of starting to invest regularly as early as possible, preferably in your early 20s. No, it's not convenient, but through the magic of compound interest, it makes a world of difference. And if you're well past that prime period to start this magic, teach this to your kids so they don't miss it.

Albert Einstein once said that compound interest, not $E=mc^2$, "is the greatest mathematical discovery of all time." As usual, he's right.

THE RULE OF 72

You can calculate the number of years it will take to double your money by using "The Rule of 72." Simply divide the interest rate into 72, and the answer is the number of years for your investment to double. This works, of course, no matter how much money is invested, but it doesn't take taxes into consideration. For example, if you have an account that is earning 8%, you divide 8 into 72, and you find that it will take 9 years for your money to double.

RISK EARLY, NOT LATE

Some people who come to see me are in their 50s, and they are desperate to make as much money in a few years before they hope to retire. They want me to put their money into high risk, and hopefully high yield, investments. A better way to look at it is to realize that higher risks make sense only for the long haul. Historically, the market has trended up over long periods of time, but it reacts with alarming volatility in short time spans. A casual glance at a graph of the Dow, S&P, or NASDAQ indices demonstrates these facts. For that reason, financial planning professionals generally recommend investments with lower risks for shorter time horizons, but if you can keep your money in place for a long time, you can ride out the ups and downs of the market and take advantage of higher risk instruments with higher returns.

A young couple about 26 years old asked for my advice about investing their 403b. We talked about their goals and when they would need the money, and they agreed that they wouldn't need it until their children (yet unborn, and to their knowledge, unconceived) went to college. I recommended an aggressive growth mutual fund.

A couple in their 50s had a different look in their eyes. Instead of curiosity and confidence, panic filled their faces and voices. "I need to make as much as I can as quickly as I can," the husband assured me.

"We don't know what might happen," his wife agreed.

I explained the principles of risks and time horizons, and reluctantly, they decided to invest in funds with less risk but greater stability. That proved to be a good choice because the market went down about the time she had major surgery and they needed to withdraw some of the funds. Choosing the lower risk investment saved them about $8000.

THE PERFECT INVESTMENT

Well, there may not actually be a "perfect" investment, but matching funds come as close as anything I've ever seen. Many companies offer to match money we put into retirement accounts, and that's free money! It doubles your income immediately, and it will multiply your savings over time.

Sadly, I've known a number of people who didn't take advantage of this incredible opportunity. If your employer offers it, do whatever you need to do to get the maximum you can get. You might not be able to afford the latest gadget for your computer every time a new one comes along, but you'll have something far better: peace of mind that your future is looking good!

Don't Handcuff Your Kids with Handouts

We love our children, and we want to show it. Some of us show it by giving them lots of money, but the effects can be quite the opposite of our intentions. Instead of providing wings for them to fly, those funds handcuff them to the ground.

Not all gifts of money shackle our children. We can use gifts of money to stimulate responsibility. For example, some parents offer to match dollar for dollar the money their children earn toward buying a car. That can have a very positive impact on a young person by teaching the fact that discipline and hard work yield rewards.

Too much of a good thing—large gifts without expectations of responsibility—can genuinely harm our kids. In their study of millionaires, Stanley and Danko made a number of observations about parents who give money to their children. In retrospect, these conclusions seem to be obvious, but many wealthy parents don't realize the negative impact they have by giving too much. Stanley and Danko found that receiving cash gifts produces kids whose lifestyle is characterized by consumption rather than saving and investing, and these kids become emotionally and financially dependent on their parents, often well into adulthood and until their parents die.[21]

Too much of a good thing—large gifts without expectations of responsibility—can genuinely harm our kids.

---

21 Thomas J. Stanley and William D. Danko, *The Millionaire Next Door*, (Simon & Schuster, Pocket Books, New York, 1996), pp. 153-159.

Why do some parents give their kids too much? There are several possible answers. Some parents experienced hardships when they were young, and they simply want to protect their children from those difficulties. Other parents feel guilty that they haven't been the mothers and fathers they know they should have been, and they try to compensate by giving cash and presents. Similarly, some parents try to buy their children's love, or they may try to use money and lavish gifts to make their kids happy. The questions we need to ask are:

- Am I giving money or things primarily for them or for me, to make me feel better as a parent because I've blown it so badly?

- Will this gift build or destroy my child's sense of independence and responsibility?

In some cases, parents who have been giving too much to their kids for a long time have developed children with a debilitating, deep-seated dependence. Changing course at this point requires far more courage and communication than would have been necessary if they had changed directions earlier, but it's still worth it. It's never too late to wean a dependent child from his parents. The process may be painful, but it simply must be done if you want your children to become emotionally healthy adults.

Ultimately, personal maturity, growth, and wisdom are stunted in young people who receive too much from their parents. Self-absorption ruins relationships, distorts purpose, and crushes drive that leads to achievement. Irresponsible adult children—that's not a legacy any of us want to leave to our families. Teaching our kids some of these small steps early in life has a huge payoff for them and for us. (We'll look at a lot more on this topic in Chapter 8.)

Give 'Em Choices

Since we're talking about children, Buck and Jeeta are friends who taught their son Todd valuable lessons about money by giving him simple, meaningful choices. When they went out to eat as a family and the waiter asked for their drink order, they asked Todd, "Do you want a Coke, or do you want a dollar?"

Jeeta told me, "Todd's pretty smart. He picked the dollar every time."

Buck and Jeeta found a teachable moment, and they used it over and over again to show their son that simple choices make a difference.

The Snowball Effect

When people who are buried in debt decide it's time to make a change, they often look at their list of debts, wince a time or two, and prioritize from the largest to the smallest. That's the wrong way to do it. Financial planning professionals recommend that you start with the smallest debt and work toward the largest. When the first one is paid off relatively easily, the sense of accomplishment propels you to the next one, and the next, and the next. They call this "the snowball effect."

I've seen this effect many times with my clients and friends. Those who tried to pay off their biggest debt often became discouraged when it took so long to see any real progress—like no more demand letters from that creditor! In some cases, they simply quit trying. But I've also seen plenty of people start with their smallest debt and experience genuine joy when they make their last payment on it. They were highly motivated to take on the next challenge.

If you think this sounds like pop psychology, that's fine. You probably aren't in debt and don't need the adrenaline boost of joy to keep you going as you deal with tons money you owe.

Dress for Success

My wife Connie is a smart shopper. We live on a budget, and part of that budget is her clothes allowance. Long ago, she found a way to beat the system. She realized that many upscale women's resale shops have clothes she loves for a fraction of the price in department stores. These days, she feels like she's splurging when she buys a couple of dresses in a month. They cost about $25 each instead of $150 or $200, so she comes out like a bandit!

Two for One

When Connie and I were poor, we sometimes went to nice restaurants and bought two meals. We seldom could eat everything on our plates (well, Connie couldn't), but that, we were sure, was the price of going out to eat. Somewhere along the way, however, we realized that portions were so big that we could easily split a dinner and save a lot of money. For the past 15 years, we've seldom ordered two meals. We always have plenty to eat, and if we're still hungry, we go wild and get dessert.

Some people think that splitting a dinner somehow shortchanges waiters who have to do the same amount of work for half the tip. We solve that by giving a larger tip, so everybody's happy.

How much have we saved over the years? My estimate is that Connie and I go out to eat three times a week. (Yes, I know that's a lot.) If we save an average of $12 on each meal, that's $36 a week and $1872 a year. Over the 15 years, that comes to over $28,000 (with no interest on the money)! If we had paid that much each time, I'm not sure we'd have gone out to eat as much, or maybe we'd have gone to restaurants with cheaper meals. Even if we didn't save that much money, we went to nice restaurants, enjoyed fine meals together, and stayed within our budget. That works for us!

The Real Cost of a Cup of Coffee and a Car

I want to give you a fresh perspective about the real cost of drinking specialty coffee and driving new cars. In this exercise, let's assume that the money you save is invested.

Many of us go to coffee shops every day and buy a cup of specialty coffee, latte, or one of those iced coffee drinks. The cost varies, but let's assume that we spend $5 each visit on the drink, and occasional brownie, and a tip for the barista. Five visits a week at $5 a visit is $25 a week or about $1200 annually. If you're 25 years old, and you save that money and put it into a mutual fund that grows 10% a year, when you're 65 you'll have $531,111. (Connie didn't believe me when I gave her the total, so she got her pencil and did the math herself. Now she's convinced!)

> *When you're 65, that $200 a month at 10% interest will have become a whopping $1,062,222!*

Now, let's assume that you start leasing a BMW convertible when you're 25 and you pay $400 a month for the lease. That's $4800 each year. Now let's assume that you learn to value your future more than your fine ride today, so you decide to spend $200 a month on a small Toyota or Honda and invest the rest. When you're 65, that $200 a month at 10% interest will have become a whopping $1,062,222!

INTENTION

The wisest man on earth had a lot to say about financial planning. Even a casual reading of the Proverbs shows us that Solomon understood the importance of having a clear, intentional plan for handling money. Throughout his statements in Proverbs and Ecclesiastes, he reminds us that a plan helps us make good choices, and those choices make a difference—a big difference. He wrote, "Careful planning puts you ahead in the long run; hurry and scurry puts you further behind" (Proverb 21:5).

Small steps in the right direction, he assures us, eventually take us places we want to go. He observed, "Work your garden—you'll end up with plenty of food; play and party—you'll end up with an empty plate. Committed and persistent work pays off; get-rich-quick schemes are rip-offs" (Proverbs 28:19-20).

In the study of wealthy people in *The Millionaire Next Door* and in my observations of people who have attained both financial and relational wealth, we see that seemingly small steps of planning and choices to be frugal in spending are two of the hallmarks of people who accumulate real wealth. That's not a secret. We can all apply these basic lessons of life.

THINK ABOUT IT...
1. On a scale of 0 (nada) to 10 (the max), rate your need to address each of these small steps in your life. (Each of these is independent, so you don't have to rank them in order. Each can be any number that fits.)

—The magic of compound interest

—Risk early, not late

—The perfect investment

—Don't handcuff your kids with handouts

—Give 'em choices

—The snowball effect

—Dress for success

—Two for one

—The real cost of a cup of coffee and a car

2. Which of these have been modeled to you by your parents or friends? How has that modeling shaped your decisions?

3. Look back and the numbers for the real cost of a cup of coffee and a car. Do these figures motivate you to make any changes in your consumption? If so, would you use the money you save on other purchases you'd like to make, or would you save and invest that money? Explain your answer.

4. Have you taken any small steps that resulted in big payoffs? If you have, describe them.

GOING DEEPER

1. Read Proverb 21:5. How have you seen financial planning help people get ahead or the lack of planning put people behind? Who are some examples of each one? (No names, please!)

2. Read Proverbs 28:19-20. How have you seen "committed and persistent work" pay off in someone's life (especially your own)?

3. What are some reasons some people fail to connect the dots about the value of planning and the benefits of persistence?

7 | Tipping Points

"Courage is being scared to death—but saddling up anyway."
—John Wayne

Several years ago, Connie, Carissa, Brandon and I went skiing in Colorado with several families from our community. No one in our family had ever skied before, but from the first day, we had a blast! At the end of the second day, I was taking one last trip down the mountain. I hit a patch of ice and took a tumble, and a stump arrested my fall. My chest hit it at full speed! It knocked the breath out of me, and I was pretty shaken. In only a few seconds, the pain was so bad that I thought they'd have to call for a helicopter rescue. I gasped for breath, and my chest felt like every rib was broken. I thought, *If I live through this, it'll be great. And if I'm able to walk again, it will be a miracle!* I was as scared as hurt. After about 15 minutes, I was able to move a little bit. I was bleeding and bruised, but not on the verge of seeing my Maker like I'd feared. That was it for me. No more skiing that year.

The next winter, the same crowd of friends planned a trip to go skiing again. The memory of my last run the previous year haunted me, but I didn't say a word. Connie and the kids had had a wonderful time the year before, and all summer and fall we talked about making an annual trek to the mountains to ski. This was the first thing our family had been excited about doing together, and I didn't want to mess it up. By the time we got to Colorado, though, I was having panic attacks: rapid, shallow breathing, sleeplessness, nausea, and sheer terror at the thought of getting hurt again. My insides were in a knot, but I didn't want to tell anybody because I was ashamed.

I desperately wanted to have fun with my family and friends, and in that moment of need, I told my friend George about my fears. He didn't laugh at me, and he didn't tell me I was stupid. He just listened, and then he said, "Hey, why don't you and I ski together?" It was one of the most gracious things anybody has ever done for me.

My anxiety, though, didn't disappear in that moment. It was too deep to be washed away by a kind word from a friend. As George went down the mountain with me, I fell over and over again because I was so tense, and I threw up several times. (Sounds like fun, huh?) After a few minutes, George came to my rescue. He gave me a new perspective about what I was trying to do. He said, "Instead of just pointing your skis downhill, pick a point across the slope, ski to it, and then pick another point back across the slope. Manage the mountain from one point to another."

The combination of George's kindness and his lesson on a new strategy made a world of difference. By the time I got to the bottom of the slope, I had renewed hope that I could enjoy skiing with my family for years to come. What a relief! And that was just the first run of the day. George hung out with me the rest of the day, and he showed me more techniques and helped me understand more of the art of skiing. By the end of the day, my confidence had soared!

The last three years, our family has gone skiing each year, and we've had some of the best times of our lives. Today, I look back on that moment when I first talked to George about my fears, and I'm so thankful for his friendship, encouragement, and instruction.

My experience skiing parallels how a lot of people think and feel about financial plans. They may not throw up and have panic attacks, but they feel overwhelmed and paralyzed by the fear that they'll make a mistake. All of us need to be honest with a friend who can step into our lives and give us some encouragement and direction. We may not be able to figure it all out on our own, but we don't have to. A friend can help us take the first step, and when we see success, we'll be able to take another and another. Soon, we're connecting our resources to what matters most, and we're skiing down the proverbial black slope in our finances.

Tipping points are moments of choice. In those moments, we can stay stuck in neutral, or we can make courageous decisions—however much we hesitate in making them—to take a step toward our goals.

> *Tipping points are moments of choice. In those moments, we can stay stuck in neutral, or we can make courageous decisions.*

CRITICAL MOMENTS

Early in the book, we identified four types of people and how they manage money. People in each category come to a moment of choice when they either move forward or stay stuck in a rut.

- Many people who are buried in debt have continued to make poor decisions because they don't want to face painful realities. Robert and Joyce had made countless bad decisions over the years, and now in their 50s, they found themselves with a mountain of debt and virtually no assets. They owned their home, but they had borrowed on the equity every time the market went up a few thousand dollars. Four credit cards were maxed out, and they owed more on their cars than they were worth. By the time they came to see me, creditors had been calling for six months, and they faced a torrent of demand letters.

Joyce had seen it coming for years, but Robert always made excuses and laughed off any problems. Now, though, Joyce wasn't willing to listen to Robert's lies any longer. She insisted that they get help. "If you won't face the facts," she growled at him in anger, "I'm going to leave you. You can count on it!"

That did it. Robert never imagined that their financial problems would come to that, but Joyce simply couldn't handle the multiple strains of financial stress and relational discord. Something had to give. (She thought about murder, but she ruled it out.) Leaving him would at least give her some distance so she could reclaim her life. The look in Joyce's eyes told Robert that this time, her threat was real. He told her, "I don't know what to do, but I'll call Jim. Maybe he can help us."

Immediately, Robert called me, and in an hour, he and Joyce sat in my office pouring out their hearts. Robert obviously felt very uncomfortable, especially when Joyce's anger flared several times. But he took it like a man. After we talked for a while, I outlined a simple plan to move them toward the black. Robert listened carefully. At the end, I asked, "Robert, are you willing to commit yourself to this plan?"

He looked me in the eyes and said simply, "Whatever it takes." And he meant it.

The road for them has been difficult, but they're making really good progress. Tune in a few months from now, and I think you'll see that they're completely out of debt. But that's only part of the story. Robert's new honesty has opened the doors that his denial had closed in his relationship with Joyce. They aren't out of debt yet, but they're happier than they've been in years.

Joyce told me recently, "I feel like we've gotten our lives back."

- Joseph and Rachel had been married only a few months, but they instinctively knew they needed to look to the future. Rachel's father had drilled into her that financial planning brings relief, peace, and options that aren't available to those who fail to plan, so she was ready to talk about their financial future. Joseph's parents had very modest means and had lived barely above water all their lives, but Joseph wanted more for Rachel, and for the children they hoped to have one day. He, too, was eager to look forward. They came from different experiences, but

> *Financial planning brings relief, peace, and options that aren't available to those who fail to plan.*

they reached their tipping points through wonderful conversations about God's plans for their future.

Both Joseph and Rachel worked, but neither of them made much money. Investing in their family's future would require considerable sacrifice, but they weighed the alternatives and made some hard choices. Both of them worked for companies that offered matching funds for their 401ks, so Joseph and Rachel signed the papers to invest the maximum their company would allow, and they put their money in aggressive growth funds.

They came to me with some questions a few months later, and they told me what they had done. I smiled and told them, "You did exactly the right thing. You guys are really sharp!"

• Several years ago, I was the classic example of bucks in the bank, but still worried. I had devoted my life to being a successful businessman, and I made a lot of money, but I felt strangely empty. One summer, I went with my son Brandon and our church on a mission trip to Haiti to build a church there. One morning I was on the roof of that little church cleaning the worksite with some friends and a few Haitian boys who had joined us. One of the boys came up to me and quietly said something in Creole. I couldn't understand him, but he kept saying the same thing and pointing to my fanny pack. I yelled to a friend, "Hey Steve, what's this boy saying to me?"

Steve walked over and knelt down with his face to the little fella so he could hear him, then he turned to me with a pained expression and said, "He's hungry, Jim. He wants you to give him the crackers in your pack."

That moment on the roof that morning was a tipping point for me. I had made plenty of money, but my life was empty. Here was a human being with desperate needs that I could meet with ease. I had lived my life with me in the center, on the throne, and in neon lights, but now I saw that God had given me resources that I could use to touch people's lives. It was only a pack of crackers, but it was something I had that could make a difference. As I handed crackers to a hungry little boy that day, I knew my life would never be the same.

- People who are full of purpose and contentment arrived at their tipping point years before. Some had been taught valuable lessons when they were kids, and they made good choices early in their lives. Many others, though, lived for years deeply in debt, barely in the black, or fairly wealthy but without a sense of purpose. At some point, however, they realized that money, stuff, and hard work are all valuable up to a point, but life is about much more than things. It's about people and purpose. They came to a point of decision, and they made a wise choice.

In an earlier chapter, we looked at Jesus' parable about the soils, and we saw that the weeds of worry, deception, and greed have choked out the spiritual vitality of many people. Many of us have been choked like that, but at a point in time, we realized that we had a choice to go in a different direction and experience a life of joy, peace, and contentment. Today, people who are full of purpose and contentment still are tempted by worry, deception, and greed, but they see the weeds and take initiative to pull them before they choke their lives.

Why No Change?

Why do some people recognize their choices and make decisions that enhance their lives, but others fail to see choices, or see them and fail to act? There may be many different reasons, but I want to highlight a few.

Lack of information

I've talked to a lot of people of all ages who simply didn't have any background in financial issues, so they weren't aware of their options in managing their money. Some of them had seen countless ads about investments, but for some reason, they always thought they were for somebody else. A little information, though, can work wonders. Many of these people devoured the booklets and charts I gave them, and they scoured the web sites I sent them to—and they learned what they needed to know to make good decisions with their money.

The wound

I know people who experienced the devastating trauma of abuse, the emotional scraping of habitual criticism, or the gnawing pain of abandonment. These wounds affect every area of our lives, including how we manage money. They distort our ability to perceive things accurately, and they drive us to take big risks to hit it big and *prove* ourselves, do whatever others want to *please* them and earn approval, or *hide* from any form of risk to protect ourselves from hurt again. Wounded people have additional hurdles to overcome, but I've seen many of them face their hurts with courage and learn life's richest lessons about love, life, and money. These men and women learned the hard way, but they learned.

> *These wounds affect every area of our lives, including how we manage money.*

When we've been deeply hurt, we feel like victims, talk like victims, and act like victims. Victims blame others for their problems, and they remain paralyzed, unwilling or unable to take steps forward. Certainly, an honest assessment of our lives includes the fact that we've been hurt, and we can then grieve the losses, forgive the offender, and move on with our lives. Some people prefer the convenience of blaming others rather than taking responsibility for their futures. Moving forward takes a lot of courage, but it's the path of healing and growth.

Shame

Some of us have given up. In the past, we may have tried to make life work, but we failed. Or maybe we never tried at all. For some reason, we feel hopeless and helpless, letting life just pass us by. People who feel ashamed focus their attention on themselves, but they sure don't like what they see! Their view of life is, "Nothing will ever go right, and if I try, I'll just mess things up." They put on masks to try to look happy and competent so nobody will know what's really going on inside, but the gloom of shame doesn't result in a positive, future oriented, purposeful life (or an effective financial plan).

No vision for the future

I've known some people who were so absorbed in having fun today that they don't think beyond the next party, the next cruise, or the next ski trip. They want all they can get, and they want it now. To them, money is only valuable if it meets their immediate desires. I've known a few of these people who lied, stole, and cheated to get what they want.

Sure, we can all find excuses to explain why we do the dumb things we do, and I've either heard or used most of the ones about neglecting to do any financial planning. But when I think of these excuses, I remember a single mom who charted a course for her son's future even though she has very modest means, or a couple with a disabled child who found resources they (and I) never knew existed, or a lady whose husband had a heart attack when he was in his mid-40s, without disability and with no income for months. She looked at the reality of their situation, found the help she needed, and boldly made decisions that kept their family on solid financial ground. Heroes all.

STEPS OF CHANGE

I hope you've already taken some steps forward to identify your purpose and connect your resources to what matters most, but in case you need a bit more encouragement, I want to offer some perspectives that may help. As I've thought about my own struggles and the struggles of friends and clients, I've noticed seven steps we can take.

Honesty

For a traveler who's lost, the first step is to find out where he is. As long as he refuses to admit he's lost, he'll keep going in the wrong direction. For years, I honestly thought that devoting my life to success in my career was the right thing to do. I didn't wake up each morning and think, *Today, I'm going to ruin myself and my family by pursuing the wrong purpose.* But that's exactly what I did.

In the last few years, I've learned to value honesty as one of the highest virtues. It's hard for most of us to be really truthful with ourselves or with someone else (especially our spouse), but it's the necessary first step in finding purpose and reclaiming a life that's out of control.

As I've talked to people about the process of change, some of them have commented that they are afraid of losing control. But in most cases, their perception of the threat is an illusion. Many of them think they actually have control of their lives, but they are spiraling out of control, hurting the ones they love and robbing them of the happiness and fulfillment they long for. In reality, we are only in control when we have a purpose, a plan, and a strategy to accomplish what matters most to us. Some people think a budget is too constricting, but a friend of mine told me that his budget gives him incredible peace and freedom because he doesn't have to worry about money all day, every day.

A young couple, Brian and Alicia, told me that when they were in pre-marriage counseling, the counselor asked them to tell each other the thing they most feared. They were terrified to be so painfully honest with each other, but they swallowed hard, looked at each other, and spoke the truth about secret fears that had haunted them. Brian told me, "I really didn't want to tell Alicia those things, but as soon as a I did, I realized that now she knew the worst about me, so I didn't have to be afraid any more. She knew, and she still loved me. Being honest with each other has given us incredible freedom to enjoy each other."

Honesty can do the same thing for each of us, if we speak the truth about money: our hopes, our fears, our secrets, and our new commitments.

Hope

Genuine hope can be a slippery and elusive thing. Some people have been hurt or they've failed badly in the past, and they have

> *True hope blends a rigorous grasp of reality with tenacious optimism.*

given up all hope, but on the other end of the scale, some divorce hope from reality and believe that things will somehow magically work out without having to deal with the painful truth. True hope blends a rigorous grasp of reality with tenacious optimism.

Admiral James Stockdale was the highest-ranking American prisoner of war in Viet Nam. For years, he languished in the "Hanoi Hilton," his days alternating between boredom and torture. Days turned to weeks, weeks turned to months, and months turned to years. Through those long, mind-numbing, hope-killing years, Stockdale waited to be rescued, but until the war was over, American soldiers never came. In his book, *Good to Great,* author Jim Collins recalls a conversation he had with the Admiral many years after the war. Stockdale talked of his commitment to be realistic about his situation as a POW, and Collins asked, "Who didn't make it?"

"The optimists," Stockdale replied.

Collins was surprised. He wondered, *Wouldn't optimism be a necessary trait for a prisoner to hang on to?*

The Admiral explained that "the optimists" were those who clung to the hope that they'd get out of prison by the next Christmas. When that didn't happen, they believed they'd get out by Easter. When that didn't occur, they convinced themselves they'd be freed by a certain date in the summer. Sooner or later, the disappointment of unfulfilled expectations eroded their ability to make it through another day of confinement and torture. Many of these men died in prison of a broken heart. Stockdale faced the same torment and loneliness, but he held tightly to two perspectives: Retain faith that you will prevail in the end regardless of the difficulties, and at the same time, confront the most brutal facts of your current reality, whatever they may be. Collins calls this dual perspective on hardship "The Stockdale Paradox."[22]

---

22 Jim Collins, *Good to Great,* (Harper Business, New York, 2001), p. 86.

Most of us tend to drift to one side and exclude the other, either being *overwhelmed with the pain and disappointment* in our lives, without hope that any solution is even possible, or we live on the other end of the continuum, *having blind faith* that "everything will be just fine" and hoping that someone, somewhere, somehow will magically solve our problems. Both ultimately lead to discouragement and self-pity; one simply gets there faster. The Stockdale Paradox applies perfectly to people who struggle with finances, especially those who are buried in debt. We have to be brutally honest about our current situations, and retain faith that we eventually will see the light of day—the end of debt and a life of purpose and contentment.

Our hope, though, ultimately isn't in our finances. It needs to be rooted in a higher reality. For many years, I put my hope in business success and money, but it led to strained relationships, distorted thinking, enormous stress, and debilitating depression. I found that I needed to focus on a reality that's a lot bigger—on a transcendent reality . . . on God. He gives perspective, strength, and forgiveness. He's the source of genuine hope.

Paul is a young man in his 20s who loves to talk to people about his faith in God. He told me about his conversation one day with a student from China. They had gotten to know each other when a mutual friend introduced them at a coffee shop, and they soon learned that they both were fans of music and technology. They talked about bands they enjoy, and they talked about web sites where they could find obscure music downloads. After a while, the conversation naturally turned to more meaningful things. Paul asked the student some questions about his background. In China, people are taught atheism, but many of them long to know a higher being. The student asked Paul to explain how he could know the God Paul was talking about. Paul started explaining the story of Jesus, and the student became strangely quiet. Their relationship had been brief, but it was strong enough for Paul to ask, "What's wrong? Did I say something that offended you?"

The student looked at him and said, "No, you say that God offers me forgiveness and life. I want that so much, but I'm afraid I will lose control of my life."

A week later, Paul and the student met again to talk about Christ. He told Paul he had been thinking about God all week, but he was still struggling with the concept of putting God on the throne of his life. Paul told him, "If you put your life in Jesus' hands, you'll *find* your life."

Somehow, that made sense to him. The student understood that the benefits of putting God at the center of his life far outweighed the risks. They talked a little longer, the student told Paul that he wanted to put his trust in Christ. Then Paul asked, "Are you willing to put Christ on the throne of your life?"

"Yes," the student responded, "I'm telling him that right now."

Hope comes in many different packages, but sometimes, our hope is fixed on things like money, success, and pleasure that can't fill the God-sized hole in our hearts. Jesus promised to forgive us and make us fully alive if we trust in him, and he said he'd give us peace—his peace—in the middle of life's most difficult times. We are fully human, but we long for the touch of the eternal. We long for God—our source of hope in the best times and the worst times, times of plenty and times of need.

> *Jesus promised to forgive us and make us fully alive if we trust in him, and he said he'd give us peace—his peace—in the middle of life's most difficult times.*

You may be thinking, *I've made such bad decisions for so long that I don't have much hope that things will ever change.* But you have enough. You wouldn't have read this far in this book if you didn't have at least some hope that you can take some steps, change directions, and find the peace of mind and sense of purpose you've longed for. And "some hope" is enough to keep going.

Courage

Courage isn't the absence of fear; it's taking action in spite of our fear. Let's face it—life is complex, and nothing is assured. There are no sure-fire investments, and no one can guarantee tomorrow for any of us. People who demand guarantees are often paralyzed because they are afraid to take any risks, but life is full of risks. We certainly don't want to take foolish risks, but we need to embrace the adventure of life, and adventures necessarily involve some risks.

I've met with hundreds of people and helped each of them design a financial plan based on what matters most, their current situations, and their goals. But that's not enough. To get to those goals, each of them has to take steps to write checks, not spend too much, and take the specific steps toward the future they've envisioned. Most of these people have the courage to take those steps, but some are like a skier who gets his gear and skis on, buys a lift ticket, rides to the top of the mountain, and stands at the top of the slope . . . and stands and stands and stands. If people with financial plans don't push off and head down the mountain, they can avoid risk, but they miss out on all the joy, fun, and thrill of seeing their life's goals fulfilled.

Every time we muster the courage to take a step, we develop that most precious commodity: character. And as we take step after step, we realize that even more opportunities wait for us—like going from a green slope, to blue, to black, and maybe even to black diamond!

Trust

I see commercials for online brokerage companies that promise "independence" for people who want to invest on their own. That may be fine for somebody with years of experience in designing, fine-tuning, and implementing a financial plan, but most of us need a trusted friend to help us clarify our choices and give us a little encouragement to do the right thing. In fact, I'd say that having a person we can trust is absolutely essential to the process of financial management.

I want to warn you about people who are more interested in selling products and earning commissions than in helping you fulfill your dreams. I've known people like that, and for a while, I saw one in the mirror each morning! Fee-based financial planners are paid to objectively analyze your situation and make recommendations with no pressure to sell products that aren't part of your goals.

Some of us need to hire a professional to help us design a financial plan, but most of us can get far down the road with a little time, a little diligence, and a friend who can help us because he or she has already gone down that road.

If you wonder if your financial planner has mixed agendas, here are some things to watch for:

- Is he wearing a Rolex and Bruno Magli shoes?

- Is she driving a $90,000 car, but you caught her talking about having a hard time paying her credit card bill?

- Does he charge a fee, or is he paid by commissions from sales?

- Does she appeal to your selfish side, focusing on the indulgence you can enjoy if you have a lot of money, or does she ask about what matters most to you?

- Does his offer seem to be prepackaged, one-size-fits-all?

- Does she use any pressure to get you to buy a product?

- Is he as slick as the proverbial used car salesman, always smiling and promising, glossing over details and moving in for the check?

To find a professional you can trust, ask friends to tell you about the professionals they use, and look for someone who is genuinely interested in his or her clients' goals. Interview two or three before you decide. (You may find that a friend's perception of his professional is very different than yours!) Don't settle on someone until and unless you're convinced he or she values what matters most to you, doesn't use slick presentations, and doesn't over-promise. Remember that the professional's role is to give you advice and assistance, but you retain responsibility and control of your decisions. Don't invest in anything unless you clearly understand the risks and potential rewards. In other words, every time you commit resources, the investment and risk has to make sense. You can try a professional for a while, but you aren't married to this person. If, at some point, you don't feel that your visions for your financial future are compatible, or if the professional seems to forget what matters most to you, find someone else.

Trust is the most important ingredient in any relationship. If you've found someone who can help you chart the course for your financial future, treasure that person. If you haven't looked for that person, start looking. If you've looked but haven't found someone you trust, keep looking. Don't stop until you find someone who wants to help—with no hidden strings attached—and is genuinely concerned about what matters most to you.

"You really want this, DON'T you!?... Now quit wasting my time and SIGN HERE!!!"

Information

Some people feel uptight about financial planning because it seems so nebulous and strange, but once they get some handles on basic information, they have far more confidence. The right information is golden. We don't have to be experts in the seven areas (financial freedom, risk management, etc.), but we need a basic understanding, and we need to know where to get good information when we need it.

People's situations and their needs for information are vastly different. Someone who is buried in debt needs facts about cash flow and credit, but someone who has significant resources may have never written a will, so that's priority #1 for that person.

Brokerage houses, insurance agencies, and a host of other companies offer more information on the web than you can find time to read. Find a resource that is trustworthy, and gain insight about your choices. (In the back of this book, you'll find a brief list of some resources I recommend.)

Take action

Some err by taking action without adequate information, and others err by not taking action until they squeeze the last drop of information out of every possible resource. Each of us has to feel comfortable that we have enough facts so we can make an informed decision, but sooner or later, we have to take action if our goals are to be realized.

Each of the elements in FREETIC requires research and action, and they reward us handsomely with security, peace of mind, and confidence in the future. But those wonderful benefits don't just happen some day in the future. We have to take action now so we can reap the benefits later.

Someone who is buried in debt needs to develop a budget, cut up some or all of the credit cards, say "no" to expenses that don't fit the new course, and say "yes" to writing checks to pay off debts.

When people who are barely above water develop a plan with a purpose, they are motivated to rearrange their spending habits to put money away for an emergency fund, their children's education, weddings, retirement, and other things that matter to them.

Men and women who have significant resources, but no peace, have probably done a good job with their investments. They need to realize that the content of their hearts determines the meaning of life, not their careers or bank statements. Many of them (and I was one) sell their souls for career advancement and more income, but it's simply not worth it. New insights about what matters most bring new choices and new joys.

People who are full of purpose and contentment developed a lifestyle of pulling weeds of greed, worry, and misplaced desires.

Their purpose lines up with God's eternal purposes, and they increasingly treasure the things God values. They model good values and effective actions to their family and friends.

Adjustments

No matter how brilliantly we've written our plan, we experience opportunities and challenges in the course of life. At that point, we need to make adjustments. Some of these are very pleasant. When a child graduates from college, parents get a "raise." Ahhh, some relief, and the chance to do some things that we haven't been able to do while we've been paying for tuition and housing. We may receive a raise at work or get a hefty inheritance, or our company may hit it big in the market and we get a windfall of income. We welcome those things!

Inevitably, though, we experience painful surprises large and small that put a crimp in our plans. An unexpected bill may be as small as a $2000 home repair, or it may be catastrophic, like an accident or disease that devastates our hearts and our families. Most families go through ups and downs of employment, moving, and sicknesses of one kind or another. If we have an emergency fund, we can handle the minor surprises fairly easily, but the big ones require a significant adjustment in our expectations and the allocation of our resources.

The Power of a Thankful Heart

Tipping points are choices, and one of the most powerful choices we can make is to be thankful. Some might read the last sentence and wonder, *I thought thankfulness was a response. How is it a choice?* Good question. I believe it's both a response and a choice. Certainly, when our hearts feel grateful, our mouths find a way to express our thanks. But I know people who exhibit tenacious thankfulness, even through some of the most difficult circumstances I can imagine. I'm not talking about a foolish, Pollyanna attitude that can't see reality. No, I'm talking about the ability to push past the obvious to see the hidden, to trust that God is at work to accomplish his purposes even when we can't see his hand at work.

I know people, like Admiral Stockdale, who are painfully honest about the disappointments and setbacks they experience, but who cling to a steadfast belief that a good and sovereign God rules the universe, and he is actively involved in every detail of their lives. They aren't limited to thanking God for the blessings they see. They have developed spiritual eyes like a cat, and they trust God to work even in darkness. With that vision, they give thanks to God because they're convinced that he will work, somehow and some way, to bring meaning even in their most difficult moments. And when they experience God's blessings, these people are the first to celebrate! I appreciate these people, and I want to become more like them.

People who are buried in debt can find all kinds of reasons to grumble, blame themselves and others, and walk around with sour expressions on their faces. But they're not alone. Those who are barely above water can be devastated by even modest, unforeseen expenses, and people who have lots of money but no purpose and peace spend their time worrying instead of enjoying life.

We don't have to wait for a windfall to become thankful people. We can choose to be thankful right where we are, right now.

We don't have to wait for a windfall to become thankful people. We can choose to be thankful right where we are, right now. We've all heard the cliché, "Have an attitude of gratitude," but that choice is one of the most powerful, life-transforming decisions we can make every moment of every day.

Develop eyes like a cat, look for lots of reasons to give thanks, and choose to express your thankfulness—even when you don't feel like it—to your family, your friends, and especially to God.

A Few Suggestions

Some of us have a major tipping point when we come face to face with the reality that we've neglected good choices for a long time, and we have a lot of catching up to do. Most of us, though, have many tipping points, and at each one, we have a choice to go forward or stay where we've been. Early in life, wise people among us set a course and take action in each of the seven areas of their plan, and then they regularly assess progress and make adjustments.

Let me give you several suggestions:

- Think about the difference it will make in a relatively short time (say, three years) if you take steps forward today. Your purpose will be clearer, you'll be closer to your goals, you'll experience more contentment, tension between you and others in your family will have decreased, and you'll be thrilled to be on track with this major part of your life. That sounds pretty good, doesn't it?

- Find a friend to talk about your purpose, your plan, and your course of action. Don't try to do it on your own. Even if you are ashamed of the decisions you've made in the past—and maybe *especially* if you're ashamed—find a friend who will listen without condemning and who will give you sound advice. You may want to find a fee-based financial counselor, or you may have a friend in business or a wise neighbor who can help you.

- Take one step in the next few days. As you've looked at the seven areas of a financial plan, has any need stood out to you? Do you need to put money in an emergency fund, write a will, get adequate life insurance, open an account for your child's college fund, or something else? Be specific, and take a step soon so you can see success. Write it down so you don't forget, and tell somebody what you're going to do. A little accountability works wonders!

REPORT CARD

Near the end of his time on earth, Jesus told his followers a story about a man who entrusted his wealth to three employees before he left on a long trip. They knew he'd ask for an accounting, a report card, when he came back home. Two of the men invested the money wisely and made a nice return. When the wealthy man arrived at home, he praised them and rewarded them handsomely. But the third man wasn't willing to take any risks with the money entrusted to him. When the wealthy man asked for his balance sheet, he only made excuses. He said, "I know you have high standards and hate careless ways, that you demand the best and make no allowances for error. I was afraid I might disappoint you, so I found a good hiding place and secured your money. Here it is, safe and sound down to the last cent" (Matthew 25:24-25).

The employer wasn't thrilled with the man's excuses. He called him "wicked" and "lazy." He scolded him: "The least you could have done would have been to invest the sum with the bankers, where at least I would have gotten a little interest" (verse 27). He took the money from the lazy employee and gave it to one of the other men. Then, like Donald Trump, on *The Apprentice,* he looked at the underachiever and said, "You're fired!"

All three employees came to a tipping point when their employer gave them responsibility for his money and walked out the door. At that moment, they faced a decision to either take a risk to move forward or to slink back in fear and laziness. Their decisions produced results that were as different as night and day. The two who got right to work were rewarded in every way, but the one who was unwilling to take a risk suffered shame, loss, and isolation.

When I read this story, I ask myself a couple of questions: What's the difference between the two that took action and the one who didn't? And where do I see myself in this story?

THINK ABOUT IT...

1. What is your definition of "tipping points"?

2. In what way does my experience skiing parallel the dilemmas and choices many people face with their finances? In other words, what are some similarities between my story and the tipping points many people face with their money?

3. Of the reasons some people don't change, which one(s) have you seen in the lives of friends and family members? Have you seen any of them in your own life? Explain your answer.

4. Explain "The Stockdale Paradox" and how it applies to making changes in how we handle finances.

5. The seven steps of change are more or less progressive, from honesty to adjustments. Where would you say that you are in taking those steps? Put a check on the continuum:

Honesty…Hope…Courage…Trust…Information…Action…Adjustments

Describe your next step.

6. In what way is the choice to give thanks a tipping point? How would "tenacious thankfulness" change your attitude, and your relationships, and your commitment to stay focused on your purpose?

7. What do you need to enable you to take the next step? Be specific.

GOING DEEPER

1. Read Matthew 25:14-30. What's the difference between the two that took action and the one who didn't? Why do you think the third man was unwilling to take a risk?

2. Do you think the wealthy employer was too harsh, or accurate, when he called him "evil" and "lazy"? Explain your answer.

3. Where do you see yourself in this story? If you got your report card today for how you've handled your resources, what grade would you get?

4. Does the fact that you will one day stand before God to give an account of your handling of resources (and every other part of your life) motivate you? Why or why not?

8 | Pay It Forward

"And as I hung up the phone, it occurred to me he'd grown up just like me, my boy was just like me." —Harry Chapin, Cat's in the Cradle

Children are sponges. They soak up the attitudes, values, and behaviors they experience in their environment. As a dad, one of the most fulfilling things in my life is to watch my children gain wisdom and responsibility in every area of their lives, including how they handle money. I hope they're learning some of those lessons from me. If they are, it's one of the biggest gifts I can give them.

Every parent I've ever known longs to leave a powerful, positive legacy to his or her children, but other people can "pay it forward" too. Teachers, employers, pastors, leaders, and friends can impart insight and model character. Singles may be tempted to tune out in this chapter, but someday most of them will want to leave a legacy to their children, so this chapter is good preparation.

In my years working with people and their money, I've had the privilege of seeing some wonderful parents model good values for their kids. One of those parents is my friend Bill.

A Mentor-Dad and a Gracious Lady

The first time I met Bill, he came to my office with this two sons for them to get some money out of the boys' universal life insurance policy to buy motorcycles. Bill explained that they had been using the policy as a savings account. For a long time, these young men had been working to earn money, and they were saving as much as possible so they could buy the bikes.

Bill bought these policies for his sons when they were young. He or they could buy more insurance every few years, and he locked in at a very low price. Bill had taught his sons the importance of investing in the future, so they knew how much their dad had put into mutual funds for their college expenses. The life insurance policy, though, was designed to help them save money to buy something they really wanted, like the bikes.

Bill didn't give his sons rigid rules about saving and spending. Instead, he taught them principles and let them make their own decisions. He helped them understand that they could spend the dollar in their hand today, but if they invest it, that dollar could be $2 or even $10 down the road. Some parents help their children save for the next toy, but Bill gave his sons a vision of what their lives could be like if they had money to invest in their own businesses when they become adults or are financially independent when they are granddads. Now, that's a long-term perspective! But Bill didn't focus only on money. He taught his sons the value of hard work, integrity, strong relationships, and the joy of serving others. He took them on trips to homeless shelters and to build churches in far-away countries. After every trip, they came back with more insight about what really matters and more thankfulness for all they have. Bill didn't just *tell* his sons about the values they should have. He *showed* them by modeling a lifestyle of responsibility and service, and he took them places where they could see, feel, hear, taste, and smell the needs of others.

One of the chief tools Bill used to impart character to his sons was Scouting. Bill was a scoutmaster, and his sons loved their involvement in Boy Scouts. Together, they hiked, climbed, swam, and camped in remote sites around the area. The projects they performed taught them lessons about teamwork and integrity, and eventually, both sons won their Eagle awards. I have a hunch that organizations like the Scouts give parents and their kids a leg up on the rest of us, because the organizations are devoted to instilling character in their members—not merely entertaining them or winning at all costs. In Scouting, Bill helped his sons (and a lot of other boys) develop physical muscles, emotional muscles, relational muscles, spiritual muscles, and eventually, financial muscles. And these boys really appreciated their dad's investment in their lives. They're now in college, and they consider their father their best friend.

For some of us, someone other than our parents "paid it forward" to impart good values about money. Mrs. Smith did that for me. When I was 17, I desperately wanted my independence, so I left home in Michigan to attend Denver Automotive and Diesel College. My father had told me he didn't have enough to pay for a college education, so I knew I'd have to earn the money to go to a university myself. For me, being a mechanic seemed to be the best ticket to college. When I walked out the door, my father told me, "I won't be able to help you out if you need more money to live on, but I'll always buy you a ticket if you want to come back home."

I moved to Denver to go to school, and to pay the bills for rent and food, I took a job in a cafeteria. After a month or so, my finances were getting pretty tight. I wasn't sure I could pay next month's rent, so in my worried mind late at night, the unthinkable became thinkable. I began considering stealing (I called it "borrowing") money from the cash register. For a few days, it was easy. I took a few dollars, and nobody said a word. So I took a little more...and a little more. One day, the owner, Mrs. Smith, called me over to a table and asked me to sit down. I wondered if she wanted to talk about the work schedule, but she told me she knew I was stealing. I didn't deny it. Mrs. Smith didn't yell and curse. Instead, she asked me some of the most penetrating questions anyone has ever asked me. She looked me in the eye and said, "Jim, what kind of reputation do you want to have? You're only 17, and you're a long way from home. What do you want your parents to think about you?"

I wasn't sure I could pay next month's rent, so in my worried mind late at night, the unthinkable became thinkable.

Mrs. Smith's questions didn't focus on my crime; they centered on my character and my reasons for living. I realized that the real issue was my pride. I refused to call home to ask my father for money. That's the reason I was stealing. I was determined to be independent and prove myself, but my pride backfired and led me down a destructive path.

I sat in front of Mrs. Smith as a guilty man. She could have called the police and had me arrested, she could have called my parents and told them what I'd done, or she could have demanded that I repay her every cent. She did none of those things. She forgave me—completely and absolutely. She forgave my debt, and she let me keep my job. Then she said something that shocked me. She quietly and genuinely told me, "Jim, I really care about you."

I can hardly describe the impact Mrs. Smith's grace had on me. My pride melted in the warmth of her kindness. Her attitude and actions that day made me a better man, gave me new incentives to be honest, and inspired me to work hard. She motivated me to the core of my heart not to ever steal again. And today, decades later, I often think of Mrs. Smith's example as I relate to my employees and others in my life, and I think I'm a lot more gracious than I would be if Mrs. Smith hadn't been so kind to me.

THE DOG WHISPERER SPEAKS

UCLA's annual study of college freshman shows that today's teens are obsessed with having more and more possessions. Three-fourths of those surveyed said it was essential for them to be "well-off financially" so they can buy all the things they want. Strikingly, that figure is almost double the survey results from 40 years ago. In a similar poll, the Pew Research Center found that the top goal for 80% of those 18-25 years old is to get rich. David Walsh is a psychologist who leads the National Institute on Media and the Family and the author of *No: Why Kids—of All Ages—Need to Hear It and Ways Parents Can Say It*. He observes, "Our kids have absorbed the cultural values of more, easy, fast, and fun." His research found that today's parents spend 500 percent more on their kids, even adjusted for inflation, than the parents a generation ago. "A lot of parents have developed an allergic reaction to their kids being unhappy," Walsh notes.[23] Parents have played a major role in creating their kids' lofty expectations and self-absorbed demands, and parents can play a role in reversing this trend—at least in the lives of their own children.

The authors of *The Millionaire Next Door* warn that giving children too much money prevents them from developing their own abilities to earn and manage money. Those gifts of money become straightjackets. On a broader scale, parents who fail to engage children in meaningful work around the home erode their children's sense of responsibility, creativity, and drive. Stop and think about the life of an average middle-class American kid today. He has far more disposable wealth than most people in world and almost every person who lived in previous eras. She's entertained almost 24 hours a day with television, video games, and MP3 players, and she's connected to her friends at every moment of every day with her cell phone, text messaging, email, and her myspace account. She's the most plugged in person in the world, rarely turning off the sights and sounds to come up for air.

The omnipresence of technology has a powerful impact on individuals and their capacity to communicate, and especially, it has cut short many parents' time with their kids. A Wikipedia article reports that Linda Stone, formerly of Apple and Microsoft, coined the term "continuous partial attention" to describe the constant distractions of e-mail, instant messaging, cell phones, and other devices. The article reports:

"To pay continuous partial attention is to pay partial attention—CONTINUOUSLY. It is motivated by a desire to be a LIVE node on the network. Another way of saying this is that we want to connect and be connected. We want to effectively scan for opportunity and optimize for the

---

[23] Quoted in *The Houston Chronicle*, "A generation obsessed with having more stuff," by Martha Irvine, January 23, 2007.

best opportunities, activities, and contacts, in any given moment. To be busy, to be connected, is to be alive, to be recognized, and to matter. We pay continuous partial attention in an effort NOT TO MISS ANYTHING. It is an always-on, anywhere, anytime, any place behavior that involves an artificial sense of constant crisis. We are always in high alert when we pay continuous partial attention. This artificial sense of constant crisis is more typical of continuous partial attention than it is of multi-tasking."[24]

Children in our culture have very little free time. Instead, their parents often feel they are depriving their kids if they aren't shuttling them from soccer practice to violin recitals, or from midget cheerleader practice to volleyball games. Instead of learning the value of reflection and creativity, children and their parents value busyness and competition above all virtues.

Television sitcoms make children kings and queens of their homes, and the shows often depict parents as bumbling idiots who exist only to fulfill the child's whims. Too often, these caricatures find expression in real people in our homes, and fiction becomes reality. (I like to *laugh* at Raymond, but I don't want to *be* Raymond! I wonder if one leads to the other. Hmmmm.)

Since we've made children the center of the universe, it's no wonder that so many kids whine, complain, and manipulate to get what they want. They've been taught through a thousand messages that they deserve the world to give them what they want and to make them happy, but that perception creates some of the unhappiest people in the world—both the kids and their parents.

Parents genuinely want the best for their kids, but love doesn't mean doing everything, all day, every day to fulfill their every dream or giving them so much that they never have cause to complain. As parents, our chief responsibility is to love our kids so much that we do whatever is necessary to impart responsibility, wisdom, and the desire to serve others. That's a tough task. It's a lot easier to give in

---

24 http://continuouspartialattention.jot.com/WikiHome

to demands, but real love backed by genuine wisdom and strength, enabling us to become counter-culture parents, who impart character instead of giving our children what they want just because "every other kid has it."

Wise parents regularly take their families away from the noise of culture so they can spend quality time together. Even at home, they carve out time for board games, family talks, and hobbies. They sometimes even turn off the television! These parents model the values of simplicity and good communication. They work hard, but they take time to rest so they maintain balance in their lives. These are the happiest and healthiest families I know.

> *Wise parents regularly take their families away from the noise of culture so they can spend quality time together.*

Connie has taught elementary school for 20 years, and she's had lots of experience watching the impact of parents on children. One year, after only a few days into the school year, she came home and told me that a student named Betty was having trouble focusing in class. As the days and weeks went by, the picture became clearer. Connie learned that Betty's father made a lot of money, but the family was buried in debt because he bought them everything they wanted—or even imagined they wanted. Instead of teaching their kids how to manage money, Betty's parents taught them that they could have absolutely anything their hearts desired.

The lights came on for Connie one day when she asked the students to get out a pencil. The other children dug around in their backpacks for a pencil, but Betty had a dozen pink princess pencils in her pack. As the little girl looked in her backpack for a pencil, all kinds of expensive toys fell out of her pack, but little Betty was frantic because she couldn't find the one pink princess pencil she wanted to use! She cried and pouted because she couldn't have her way.

The family was distracted by all their consumption. I don't know how they interacted at home, but my guess is that it mirrored Betty's behavior at school. Because of all the expensive gadgets her parents bought her, she was unable or unwilling to focus in class, and she failed to learn the important lessons Connie was trying to teach her.

When parents don't build responsibility into little children, kids grow up to be self-absorbed teenagers and adults. Thomas is a great kid, a college student with tons of personality and talent. His father is one of my clients, and he gave Thomas some of the best electronics available, for example, a $3000 laptop to use in college. Thomas's dad wanted him to learn responsibility, but he never required his son to earn money. The results are odd and alarming. The young man treats his father's cash like it's Monopoly money, wasting it without a thought of where it came from or where it's going. But when he runs out of money, Thomas is incredibly tight. His friends are perplexed because one minute, he's buying the biggest and latest sound system, and the next, he's bumming crackers and cheese from them because he doesn't have any money to buy food.

His father talked to me about Thomas's irresponsible and irrational behavior in handling money. He shook his head and moaned, "How did he get this way? I just don't get it." Then he told me that he realized how out of balance Thomas's thinking had become when his sister asked him if she could borrow his shampoo, and he replied, "No, I have to pay for that myself." Thomas didn't connect all the expensive things his father had given him and the very small request his sister asked from him. His father's generosity hadn't made a dent in Thomas's character.

Many parents are exasperated by their children's lack of responsibility. They've tried yelling. That didn't work. They tried giving them what they expected. That worked for a while, but not long. They tried everything they could think of, but the kids still won't behave and are furious most of the time. When kids are three years old, and their parents ask them to pick up their toys, they whine and pout and then explode in anger. When they are ten, and their parents ask them to unload the dishwasher, they roll their eyes in disgust. When they are teenagers, and their parents ask them to clean their room, they make excuses and put it off over and over again. In many cases, the parents' solution is to get angry, yell louder, and threaten, but too often, without real consequences. What's the deal? Connie and I like to watch a show called "The Dog Whisperer." In almost every show, Cesar Millan observes the uncontrollable behavior of someone's dog, and then he leans over and whispers to the owner, "It's not your dog. It's you. Once you set rules, boundaries, and limitations, your dog will see you as the pack leader and gladly follow." That's good input from someone who knows animal (and human) nature.

Reversing the Drift

Our culture is a river with a strong current. We swim in the water of incredible busyness, vast amounts of disposable income, expectations of instant gratification, and gadgets that promise freedom but often consume our attention. We can't stop the flow of the river, but we don't have to drift along with it either. Swimming upstream is hard, but it's absolutely essential if we are going to impart values, responsibility, and joyful generosity to those we love. We can't stop the drift of culture, but we can stop the drift of our families.

Best-selling author and leadership guru Ken Blanchard, along with Chick-Fil-A founder Truett Cathy, capture the power of giving in their book, *The Generosity Factor*. They explain, "There is a route to genuine and enduring satisfaction, but it flies in the face of this greedy, self-obsessed culture. It's called *generosity,* and it involves freely giving our four most valuable resources—our time, talents, treasure, and touch—and receiving unimaginable riches in return."[25]

We can't impart principles of financial management in a vacuum. These principles only make sense in a broader context of responsibility, honor, and purpose. As we decide how to handle issues like allowances, expectations, chores, work, and a host of other topics, we need to ask, "How can I help my child gain wisdom and grow more responsible?" Our goal isn't to make our children happy for the

---

25 Ken Blanchard and Truett Cathy, *The Generosity Factor,* (Zondervan, Grand Rapids, Michigan, 2002).

moment by giving in to their demands and buying their love with lavish gifts. The goal is to help them take steps—often invigorating, but sometimes painful—toward becoming responsible adults who value the right things and someday model love and life to their own families.

Let me share a few things I've learned (and am still learning):

A little humility goes a long way.

About a year ago, I met a man who is known for his generosity. Barry has built a very successful business, and he has made a lot of money. He gives a lot of it to causes that have captured his heart, so I wanted to meet him to see what makes him tick. Early in our conversation, he told me that he realizes that God created everything and owns everything, and that he's just a manager of a small part of God's treasures. Barry has a reputation as a good businessman who diligently practices sound principles in his work. It is further evidence of his attitude that he wants to be the best steward he can be of his business, his relationships, and his wealth.

Years ago, when his business began making substantial profits and his own income soared, Barry could have bought all kinds of new, nice stuff, but he didn't. He continued to drive his old car, and his family stayed in the same house. He saved and invested his additional income with an eye to the future. He wanted every dime to count for something far bigger than his own passing pleasure.

> *He wanted every dime to count for something far bigger than his own passing pleasure.*

Today, Barry's sons have joined him in his business, and they are full partners, with "skin in the game," not just living on handouts from their dad. Barry has modeled a humble heart coupled with a tenacious desire for his life to count, and his sons have picked up their father's attitudes. His legacy is going strong.

One of the most important concepts each of us can learn is ownership. If we believe that all we have is ours, we'll probably spend it on our selfish desires. But if we see ourselves as managers of God's gifts to us—including our hard earned salaries, because God also gave us the talents and strength to earn that money—we'll focus on God's purposes and see ourselves as his partners. That perspective makes all the difference in the world!

Replace griping with thankfulness.

I know some people who complain about everything imaginable, and they are like a big gulp of vinegar to the people around them! But I also have the privilege of knowing some who find something to be thankful for in even the most difficult circumstances. They don't close their eyes to the occasionally brutal facts, but they have a bulldog grip on hope. I like to be around these folks. In fact, I *need* to be around them!

What do our families see in us around the house? When we cook, take out the garbage, pay bills, cut the grass, or any of the myriad of other things we do at home, do they see us roll our eyes and grit our teeth, or do they see a smile on our faces? If our kids complain about doing their chores, maybe they've picked up that attitude from us, so the first place to look for change is inside our own shirts, not theirs.

Give responsibility early.

Even small children can learn to take responsibility, and the earlier they pick up this habit, the better for everybody. Of course, we need to tailor our expectations to their abilities, but even at two years old, a child can pick up toys that he's been playing with. Sure, it's easier and quicker for the parent to do it for him, but easier and quicker isn't the goal; the goal is imparting responsibility.

Teach the value of work.

One of the best books about modeling good money management to our kids is Ron Blue's *Money Matters for Parents and Their Kids.* He notes, "I believe children must experience the benefits of working early in life. In other words, when they are required to work, they experience the intrinsic value of working and feel good about a job well done. They shouldn't be paid for every job they do around the house. Work has a benefit, in and of itself, that is above and beyond the economic benefit of working; and it is important, as a part of the training process, for them to experience this benefit. It can only happen if they are required to work, doing chores around the house, without receiving pay."[26]

Link allowances to responsibilities.

Parents sometimes ask me about the value of giving a child an allowance. I think it's a very good thing to begin giving an allowance early in a child's life, as long as it's tied to realistic expectations of responsibilities that are in addition to the normal chores they perform. Some parents write up a contract: You get this much money each week, and we expect you to do these things. If they do them, they get their allowance, and if not, they get less or none at all. It's only fair, and it teaches them the immediate reward or consequences of responsibility.

> *I think it's a very good thing to begin giving an allowance early in a child's life, as long as it's tied to realistic expectations of responsibilities.*

Virtually every moment can become an opportunity to teach.

If you give your child an allowance, don't micromanage it by telling her what to save and what to spend. Explain that the money will buy this inexpensive toy today, but if she saves her money for three weeks, she can have something she really wants. Don't prod, and don't manipulate. Let the child decide. In many cases, a child will jump to get something today, but then regret the decision when she realizes what she missed by her impulsive choice. That's great! She's learned a tremendously valuable lesson that's far more powerful because she made her own choice and suffered the consequences.

---

[26] Ron Blue, *Money Matters for Parents and Their Kids*, (Thomas Nelson, Nashville, 1998), p. 57.

Have a plan to respond to whining.

Many parents don't know what to do when their children whine and complain about having to do chores or when they don't get something they want. When parents don't have a plan, they usually give in. At that point, the child realizes he's got his mom and dad right where he wants them, so he ratchets up the complaints. It's important to have a positive plan to arrest this destructive drift. A friend of mine told me that when his kids were little, their family had a rule: Whatever you whine for, you automatically don't get. What a concept! He said that his children quickly recognized that whining was counterproductive, so they learned to communicate their wants with reason instead of manipulation. The key, of course, is that my friend and his wife followed through with their commitment to deny their kids' demands when they whined, so the rule had real teeth.

Delay absorption by electronics.

Continuous partial attention is a reality in the lives of most young people today (and many adults, too). The answer isn't to move to the mountains of Montana and live like Neanderthals (though that may have its advantages). We live in the Information Age, and electronics will only get more sophisticated and omnipresent. Parents, though, can prevent their families from becoming absorbed by them by delaying the use of some electronics and carving out time for face-to-face communication in the family.

Not every five-year-old needs the latest computer, the most up-to-date video games, and the finest music and voice technology. Yes, they may complain that their friends have all these toys, but in reality, at every age, there may be only one trendsetter who everybody wants to emulate. Resist the pressure, and explain that your family values—and in fact, needs—good communication, and you aren't willing to watch your connections with each other be taken over by electronics.

For this policy to make sense, we need to carve out time to talk with each other on a regular basis. If our families aren't used to real conversation, we can play board games or cards. Try just

15 minutes three times a week, and let different people choose the game or puzzle. If you don't have anything but electronic games around the house, go to a thrift store. They often have games for about a dollar.[27]

Of course, lots of other things can absorb family time. Sports, band, clubs, and all kinds of other hobbies and activities can consume our time and prevent us from talking about the things that really matter. It's difficult, if not impossible, to impart responsibility about life and money when we can't find time to interact.

Talk about your own purpose.

Do your kids know what matters most to you? Could they articulate your purpose and values? In most families, parents either don't have clearly defined purposes or they don't find opportunities to talk about them. The kids then grow up without a clear model (or with a wrong model) to guide them to find their own purpose in life.

> *In most families, parents either don't have clearly defined purposes or they don't find opportunities to talk about them.*

Most of us wrestle with our purpose from time to time, but that's not a problem. Our children learn a lot from hearing how we wrestle with doubts and difficulties, and how changing circumstances cause us to reassess what matters most to us. Grandparents sometimes have the opportunity to share life's experiences with kids because they have a whole lifetime to reflect and clarify what has been most meaningful to them, and children sometimes listen more intently to grandparents than to parents. Nevertheless, it's

---

27 Youth speaker Mark Matlock provides encouragement for parents who want to communicate in more meaningful ways with their kids. His web site includes a long list of topics with prompts to stimulate rich family conversations. Go to www.planetwisdom.com/parents/

important for parents to play that role, too, and take initiative to share what matters most to them, even if it's not as clear as they'd like it to be. Talking about the process is just as important as sharing the end result. [28]

Talk about your money.

In an age-appropriate way, talk to your kids about the family finances. Give them perspective and understanding, but without putting the burden on them to right your wrongs and pay for debts you've incurred. You may not want talk about specific amounts of money, but from the time kids are in middle school, they can begin to grasp the seven elements of a financial plan. For instance, they'll need to know about car insurance as they anticipate learning to drive, and they'd like to know your plans for funding their college education. Depending on their age, interests, and personality, they'll grasp a little or a lot from your conversations, but it opens the door for more conversations later. One dad suggested that he and his family talk about one of the elements each night at dinner for a week. He planned to spend only a few minutes on each one, but in a few cases, the kids asked a lot of questions so the conversation lasted long after dinner.

If your family is buried in debt, share your new vision with your kids and explain why you are making changes—some of which will be painful. Ask them to support you as you dig out and pay off the bills. If your family is barely above water, talk to the kids about making some changes in spending so you can funnel more of your resources into what matters most: security for the future and causes you believe in. If your family has lots of money but lacks peace and purpose, talk about the things you're learning about the importance of having a clear mission for your life. And if your family is full of purpose and contentment, your kids undoubtedly know it. Celebrate together the privilege of connecting your resources to things that are really important.

---

28   A good resource for grandparents is the book by Phil Waldrep, *The Grandparent Factor*.

Celebrate together the privilege of connecting your resources to things that are really important.

Many families experience conflicts about money. Tension is inevitable, but we can funnel that tension into wonderful, healthy, productive conversations about vision, goals, and choices about finances. Healthy families don't shy away from taking about important things, and money is very important. Struggling families can use these conversations as steppingstones to build trust and understanding.

Have the right purpose for leaving an inheritance.

I've known some couples who's stated goal was to leave their children so much money that they'd never have to work another day in their lives. Perhaps these parents had a tough life when they were young, and they want to spare their kids the misery they suffered. Whatever the reason, I believe that goal is destructive. The Bible says it's good to leave our children and grandchildren an inheritance, but not with the goal to enable them to live self-absorbed, meaningless lives. The goal of parenting is to give "roots and wings," to impart the stability of responsibility and the joy in the adventure of life. First and foremost, we need to foster and stimulate our children's vision for a purposeful, meaningful life. Then, any money we leave them can be connected to what matters most to them.

Today, the Boomer generation is retiring, and soon, incredible wealth will pass from one generation to another. I hope these parents impart life, hope, and purpose as the foundation for using the money they leave behind.

Model frugality and generosity.

Bill, Barry, and others in this book model the twin virtues of frugality and generosity. They could buy a lot more stuff and indulge their families with a lot more pleasures, but they don't because they have an eye on the future. They live by Ben Franklin's often quoted truth, "A penny saved is a penny earned." And they use some of the money they save to give to people, churches, and causes they believe in.

In an earlier chapter, I mentioned that Connie and I learned years ago that in most restaurants, portions are so big that we can easily split a dinner. Instantly, our budget for dining out was cut in half—or more likely, we went out to eat twice as much! Over the years, our kids have watched us split meals, so it's become the norm for our family. And my guess is that they'll pass the practice along to their kids, too. But I hope that our kids also see us being generous. JR, my oldest son has worked as a busboy at Outback, and every kid who has bussed or waited tables has a sharp eye for the amount of the tip their parents leave. JR is no different. Not long ago, JR and I went out to eat after hunting with some friends. After I paid the bill, JR looked at the tip I left. It was 15%, but to him, it wasn't enough. Without a word, he pulled out a $5 bill and added it to the tip I left.

Connie and I also talk to our kids about the money we give away. Like everyone else, we receive lots of requests for donations, but our hearts aren't in them all. We try to focus our giving on our church, some missionaries, and a few organizations, and we want to give enough to make a dent in their needs. To be honest, giving to these causes is one of the most fulfilling things I do, and I enjoy talking to my family about these things so they'll share in the vision that our family is making a difference.

Being frugal doesn't mean that we pinch every penny. Saving money enables us to splurge from time to time to celebrate with our family. We take nice trips, and we go out to dinner to mark special occasions. If we didn't save money, we wouldn't have the funds to pay for these things. It's a matter of priorities, and I feel great about the choices we're making. The little decisions Connie and I make every day communicate values to our kids. In fact, those choices say more than our words ever could. Connie often gets store brands at the grocery store and saves a few cents on each item, we buy toiletries at discount stores, and I look for the cheapest gas station. Our kids are watching, and I hope they're learning good lessons.

Expose your kids to real needs.

Most of our children have no idea of the kind of poverty many people experience in our country and overseas. In the last couple of generations, millions of people moved to the suburbs to get away from homeless people, drug addicts, and crime, but in the process, we've insulated our families from exposure to the desperate needs of people who live only a few miles away. Staying in the cocoon of plenty warps our expectations and makes our hearts calloused, and we risk becoming increasingly self-absorbed.

In recent years, our church has gotten involved in a wide range of ministries to people in need. We've taken food and clothing to homeless people in downtown Houston on many occasions, and our family has participated in those efforts. Trips to other countries, though, have really changed our perspective about life. The week in Haiti shocked Brandon and me and showed us needs we never dreamed existed. Yes, we'd watched television reports about human suffering in Haiti, Darfur, Somalia, and a dozen other places around the world, but seeing it and smelling it changes everything. We all saw the devastation of Hurricane Katrina on the upper Gulf Coast, and those of us who are insurance adjusters certainly understand the level of need in those places. A group from our church, including Carissa and me, went to the Louisiana coast to help rebuild, and we were confronted by the needs of specific men and women. Suddenly, the statistics became faces. That trip spawned many rich conversations with Carissa about their needs and developed more compassion for those people in both of us.

I encourage you to invest the time and money to expose your family to desperate needs. Travel to the heart of a nearby city or the heart of Africa, but go for long enough to let the needs fill your eyes and change your heart. Those experiences are golden, providing rich talks with family members we take along, and none of us will ever forget the experience.

> **I encourage you to invest the time and money to expose your family to desperate needs.**

The Harley Life

I love motorcycles, and I love to watch people who ride them. I've seen lots of men and women (mostly men) wearing a shirt, leather vest or jacket with a Harley Davidson emblem and the city where they're from. In many cases, these emblems contain the Harley slogan: "Live to ride. Ride to live." This brief statement says volumes about their philosophy of life. They shape their lives so they can ride as much as possible, and riding gives them a rich life full of pleasure, friendship with other riders, and a sense of identity.

As we close the book, I want to paraphrase the Harley slogan and describe the philosophy I've tried to communicate in this book. As we are motivated by a compelling sense of purpose and connect our resources with what matters most, we'll gladly give our hearts, our time, and our money to meet the needs of those we love. Our philosophy is, "Live to give. Give to live." Our focus isn't on our own needs, but on the needs of others. As we devote ourselves to caring for them, we experience more joy than we ever thought possible.

"Live to give. Give to live."

In the introduction, we looked briefly at Jesus' promise that giving our hearts, time, and resources to others paradoxically makes our lives incredibly full. The more we give, the more we're filled up. He said, "Give away your life; you'll find life given back, but not merely given back—given back with bonus and blessing. Giving, not getting, is the way. Generosity begets generosity" (Luke 6:38).

There was a time when I wasn't sure that was true. I was discouraged. Some things hadn't worked out the way I hoped, and I was angry with God. But there was something about this and other promises Jesus made that I couldn't get out of my head. After a while, I told him, "Okay, God. I'll try it again. I sure don't want to be disappointed, but I trust that you're telling the truth." That moment began a gradual understanding that the paradox is true. The more I gave of my heart, my time, and my money, the more I felt filled up with peace, contentment, and the thrill of seeing my life count for something. Certainly, it's been a mixed bag. Sometimes things still don't go the way I thought they would, but God has proven that he's trustworthy, so I assume that setbacks are part of his plan, not his punishment, anger, or neglect.

The apostle Paul gives us a similar promise that good choices will bring good results. His promise is called "the law of the harvest." He wrote, "Don't be misled: No one makes a fool of God. What a person plants, he will harvest. The person who plants selfishness, ignoring the needs of others—ignoring God!—harvests a crop of weeds. All he'll have to show for his life is weeds! But the one who plants in response to God, letting God's Spirit do the growth work in him, harvests a crop of real life, eternal life" (Galatians 6:7-8).

Farmers have learned to be patient. They know that planting a seed today won't result in a crop tomorrow, but if they are patient and persistent, the harvest will eventually come. The law of the harvest is that we reap *what* we sow, *after* we sow, and *more than* we sow. When we sow kernels of corn, we reap corn, not cauliflower. When we sow love, we reap love. When we sow savings and investments, we reap multiplied income. But like a farmer, the results from our first efforts can look pretty meager for a while. It takes time for money to multiply and our kids to gain responsibility. But at some point, we can be sure that our families and our money will both grow stronger. Along the way, farmers experience seasons of fallow ground, hailstorms, frigid cold, and melting heat. The path for us isn't always smooth either, but if we're persistent, we'll see good results.

We have these two promises, from Jesus and Paul, to encourage us to take a hard look at our lives and make changes if we need to. We can find a dozen excuses to stay stuck where we are, but if we find the courage to take steps forward, we'll experience the thrill of giving our lives away so that we experience the joy of really living: Live to give. Give to live.

THINK ABOUT IT...

1. Has anyone "paid it forward" to you to model responsibility and wisdom about the important things of life? If so, explain the impact that person or those people had on you. If not, what do you think you missed?

2. Review the section about our culture ("The Dog Whisperer Speaks"). Which of the forces and trends described in this section impacts you and your family? Describe the impact.

3. Do you think it's harsh, inaccurate, or generally true to make the assumption that "It isn't the dog. It's you" in relation to parents and their kids' irresponsible behavior? Explain your answer.

4. Pick two or three of the suggestions listed and write a plan for implementing them in your family:

   — A little humility goes a long way.
   — Replace griping with thankfulness.
   — Give responsibility early.
   — Teach the value of work.
   — Virtually every moment can become an opportunity to teach.
   — Have a plan to respond to whining.
   — Delay absorption by electronics.
   — Talk about your own purpose.
   — Talk about your money.
   — Have the right purpose for leaving an inheritance.
   — Model frugality and generosity.
   — Expose your kids to real needs.

5. How do you want to "pay it forward" with your children (or employees, friends, etc.)? Describe the impact you want to have in imparting wisdom and responsibility about life, including finances.

6. Now that you've finished the book, what's your next step to make your money count? When and how will you take it?

Going deeper

1. In your own words, describe the paradox of the philosophy "Live to give. Give to live."

2. Read Luke 6:38. How have you seen this promise answered in your life and the lives of the good role models in your life?

3. Read Galatians 6:7-8. Describe the "law of the harvest." How does it apply to the principles about being a good model for others?

APPENDICES

About the Author

In almost 20 years serving his clients, Jim Munchbach has seen the power of purpose in shaping people's vision for the future, motivating them to reach their goals, and giving them a thrill when they connect their money to what matters most. Jim is the founder and president of Bridger Resources, providing coaching and training for individuals and organizations. In addition to *Make Your Money Count,* he is the author of *What Matters Most,* a book written to financial advisers who want to serve clients by first clarifying their core values. Jim's process helps professionals and their clients connect resources to what matters most.

Jim is a State Farm agent in Clear Lake, Texas, where he and his team specialize in insurance planning. His extensive experience with clients following disasters like the Northridge Earthquake, Hurricanes Andrew and Katrina, and dozens of other catastrophes has taught Jim the tremendous value of planning—*before* the unexpected happens. Jim is a CERTIFIED FINANCIAL PLANNER™ professional and he wrote *Make Your Money Count* because he believes good money management is a discipline that builds financial, emotional, as well as spiritual muscle and is a crucial element of balanced living. Jim is a lifetime member of the Christian Coaches Network.

Sound financial principles apply to people of any religious stripe: Muslim or Christian, Hindu or Buddhist, agnostic or atheist. A transcendent perspective of life, though, often comes from a person's concept of God and God's purposes for our lives. Jim is a follower of Christ, and his coaching, training, and speaking focus on helping people relate Jesus' teachings to everyday issues at work and at home, in business and in life. These lessons are intended to help individuals and families experience the hope, love, peace, and joy that Jesus promises to those who follow him.

The principles in *Make Your Money Count* are useful in business environments, civic groups, and churches. Jim is especially passionate about seeing *Make Your Money Count* used in churches—in small groups, classes, or in church-wide programs—to encourage believers to use their resources in ways that build families and honor God.

Jim and his wife, Connie, live in Friendswood, Texas, with two of their three children, Brandon and Carissa. Their oldest son, JR, serves in the United States Army. The Munchbachs belong to Friendswood Community Church, where they serve in various ministries.

About Bridger Resources

Jim Munchbach is the founder and president of Bridger Resources, which is dedicated to helping people find and fulfill their highest purposes. The company is named for one of the greatest leaders in our nation's history. Jim Bridger was known throughout the West in the 19th century as a fur trapper, mountain man, explorer, Indian fighter, and guide. Because of Bridger's assistance and focused strategies for successful travel, many settlers' dreams became reality.

Using *Make Your Money Count* and *What Matters Most,* Bridger Resources offers group training and individual coaching to help people connect their resources to their purpose. Jim is available to work with church staff, corporate executives, or community leaders who want to promote values-based financial planning. Jim's speaking engagements are tailored for a variety of interests, including personal financial planning, small group training, or professional team development.

Make Your Money Count
- Audiences: Churches (small groups and church-wide campaigns) and community groups.
- Training: Jim is available to train church staff and small group leaders to effectively communicate the principles in *Make Your Money Count.*
- Events: In addition, Jim can present this material in weekend seminars, leadership conferences, and other settings.
- Executive coaching: Many church leaders and corporate executives need individualized coaching to help them manage their resources more wisely.

What Matters Most
- Audience: Christian financial professionals and their staff.
- Training and events: Local, regional, or national workshops to equip professionals and their staff to connect with and fulfill the dreams of their clients.
- Executive coaching: In-depth assistance for execs who want to build effective teams using the principles in *What Matters Most.*

Distance Learning

Bridger Resources also offers training and coaching in a virtual learning environment which combines a tele-class system, web-based resources, and real life case studies. Our system allows you to custom design a training program that fits your busy schedule and your budget.

Contact Information

For more information about training for professionals or seminars for lay audiences, contact Jim:

- Online: www.poweredbypurpose.com

- By email: Jim@PoweredbyPurpose.com

- By phone: (281) 488-0385

- By mail: 1402 Sunset Drive, Friendswood, TX 77546

RESOURCES

Online resources to help you *make your money count:*

- Investment Planning:
  www.morningstar.com

- Finding a financial advisor:
  www.cfp.net

- Tracking your money:
  www.quicken.intuit.com

- Online brokerage service (there are many excellent online brokers, I use this one):
  www.tdameritrade.com

- Social Security:
  www.ssa.gov

- IRS:
  www.irs.gov

- Find the blue book value on a new or used car:
  www.kbb.com

- Helping students prepare for college:
  www.strenghtfinder.com
  www.aimstesting.org
  www.youruniquedesign.com
  www.planetwisdom.com

- Christian financial management:
  Willow Creek Association, Good Sense
  www.goodsenseministry.com

  Kingdom Advisors www.cfpn.org

- Coaching:
  Christian Coaches Network www.christiancoaches.com

- Books I recommend:

  What Matters Most (for financial professionals and their staff, executive coaches, small group leaders, and stewardship pastors)

  The Millionaire Next Door, Thomas Stanley and William Danko

  Renovation of the Heart, Dallas Willard

  Money Matters for Parents and Their Kids, Ron Blue

  The Call, Os Guinness

  Fully Alive, Rick Baldwin

  See Jim's site for additional resources: poweredbypurpose.com

USING *MAKE YOUR MONEY COUNT* IN GROUPS AND CLASSES

This book is designed for individual study, small groups, and classes. The best way to absorb and apply these principles is for each person to individually study and answer the questions at the end of the chapters, then to discuss them in either a class or a group environment.

The questions and exercises are designed to promote reflection, application, and discussion. Order enough copies of the book for each person to have their own. For couples, encourage both to have their own book so they can record their individual reflections.

A recommended schedule for a small group might be:

Week 1 Introduction to the material. The group leaders can tell their own stories, share their hopes for the group, and provide books for each person.

Weeks 2-9 Cover chapters 1-8, one chapter per week.

Or Prior to the first week, give out the books and ask people to prepare for the first group or class by reading the Introduction and Chapter 1.

Each of the eight weeks covers a chapter in the book.

Personalize Each Lesson

Make sure you personalize the principles and applications. At least once in each group meeting, add your own story to illustrate a particular point.

Make the Scriptures come alive. Far too often, we read the Bible like it's a phone book, with little or no emotion. Paint a vivid picture for people. Provide insights about the context of the encounters with Jesus, and help people sense the emotions of specific people in each scene.

Focus on Application

The questions at the end of the chapters and the encouragement to be authentic will help your group "get real" about their purposes and their finances. Share how you are applying the principles in the chapter, and encourage them to take steps of growth, too.

Three Types of Questions

If you have led groups for few years, you already understand the importance of using open questions to stimulate discussion. Three types of questions are limiting, leading, and open.

- Limiting questions focus on an obvious answer, such as, "What does Jesus call himself in John 10:11?" These don't stimulate reflection or discussion. If you want to use questions like this, follow them with thought-provoking open questions.

- Leading questions sometimes require the listener to guess what the leader has in mind, such as, "Why did Jesus use the metaphor of a shepherd in John 10?" (He was probably alluding to a passage in Ezekiel, but most people wouldn't know that.) The teacher who asks a leading question has a definite answer in mind. Instead of asking this question, he should teach the point and perhaps ask an open question about the point he has made.

- Open questions usually don't have right or wrong answers. They stimulate thinking, and they are far less threatening because the person answering doesn't risk ridicule for being wrong. These questions often begin with "Why do you think…?" or "What are some reasons that…?" or "How would you have felt in that situation?"

Preparation

As you prepare to teach this material in a group, consider these steps:

1. Carefully and thoughtfully read the book. Make notes, highlight key sections, quotes, or stories, and complete the reflection sections at the end of each chapter. This will familiarize you with the entire scope of the content.

2. As you prepare for each lesson, read the corresponding chapter again and make additional notes.

3. Tailor the amount of content to the time allotted. You may not have time to cover all the questions, so pick the ones that are most pertinent.

4. Add your own stories to personalize the message and add impact.

5. Before and during your preparation, ask God to give you wisdom, clarity, and power. Trust Him to use your group to change people's lives.

6. Most people will get far more out of the group if they read the book each week. Order books before the class begins or after the first week.

To Order More Copies

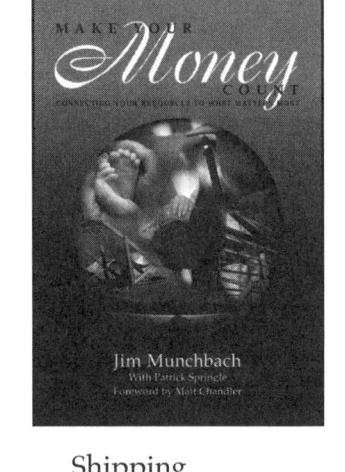

Make Your Money Count
This book is designed to be used by individuals, groups, and classes. These books also make great gifts for friends and family members who need some spiritual and financial encouragement.

Discounts and shipping

		Shipping
1 book	$24.95	$4/book
2-6 books	$22.95	$3/book
7-12 books	$20.95	$2/book
Cases of 36 books $15/book	$540.00	Free shipping

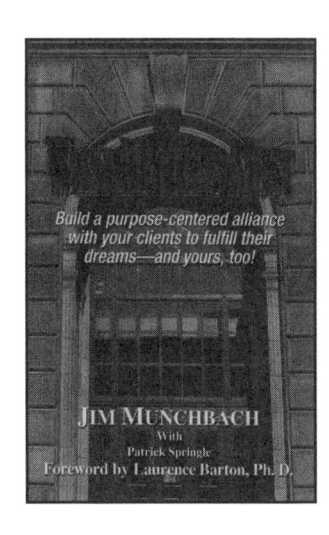

What Matters Most
This book is a tool for professionals who want to help others connect their resources to what matters most. Insurance agents, trusted advisors, stockbrokers, financial planners, tax-preparers, and anyone who provides coaching or advice in the area of money will benefit from the principles in *What Matters Most*. For more information, click on:
www.purposecenteredalliance.com

Discounts and shipping

		Shipping
1 book	$24.95	$4/book
2-6 books	$22.95	$3/book
7-12 books	$20.95	$2/book
Cases of 36 books $15/book	$540.00	Free shipping

ORDER INFORMATION

Make Your Money Count:
Number of books: _____ at $_____/book = $_____
　　　　Texas residents add 7.75% tax (x .0775) = $_____
　　　Shipping: _____ at $_____/book = $_____
　　　　　　　　　　　　　　　　　Total: $_____

What Matters Most:
Number of books: _____ at $_____/book = $_____
　　　　Texas residents add 7.75% tax (x .0775) = $_____
　　　Shipping: _____ at $_____/book = $_____
　　　　　　　　　　　　　　　　　Total: $_____

　　　　　　　　　　　　　　Grand Total: $_____

TO ORDER
Go online to poweredbypurpose.com
Or write to:
Bridger Resources
1402 Sunset Drive
Friendswood, TX 77546

Payment options: Credit cards are accepted online. Checks are accepted by mail.